The author, Dr R H Foy, is currently Secretary o
Society and a past Chairman of the Federation f
written on aspects of the history of Antrim inclu
Thompson, the old days at Carnearney and *Townlands in Ulster.*

REMEMBERING
ALL THE
ORRS

The story of the Orr families of Antrim and their involvement in the 1798 Rebellion

R.H. FOY

ULSTER
HISTORICAL FOUNDATION
LOCAL AND FAMILY HISTORY SERIES

Dedicated to the memory of Nelson and Nancy Montgomery

Published 1999
by the Ulster Historical Foundation in association with Antrim and District
Historical Society
12 College Square East, Belfast, BT1 6DD

ISBN 0-901905-95-X

Typeset by the Ulster Historical Foundation
Printed by ColourBooks Ltd, Dublin

Cover and design by Dunbar Design

Contents

Preface and
Acknowledgements

This account of the Orrs of Antrim is presented as a contribution to the history of the United Irishmen in Antrim. It evolved from a plan to mark the bi-centenary of the 1798 Rising by re-printing Francis Joseph Bigger's biography of William Orr, *Remember Orr*. Nelson Montgomery of Islandreagh, Antrim, first triggered my interest in William Orr. Nelson had been brought up beside William Orr's home at Farranshane and his brother Sydney still lives at there, while another brother, Sam, lived in the house built by William Stavely at Marymount. Stavely had attended to the spiritual needs of William Orr at his execution. Nelson had owned land in Hurtletoot where he was able to point out the wall-steads of Alex Gourley's home and Harp Hall, both of which figured in Bigger's story.

My first ambition did not extend beyond recording how these places had fared over the past 200 years, for I had assumed Bigger's account was essentially correct. But as the anniversary year loomed closer, it became apparent that Bigger's version was fired by his vivid imagination and nationalist passion rather than any great dedication to historical accuracy. In addition new avenues of research began to open up into the wider Orr family, often from chance encounters, so that a 1998 deadline became increasingly unrealistic. Any lingering obligation I may have felt to continue with Bigger was happily removed when, late in 1997, I became aware that the Linen Hall Library's United Irish Commemoration Committee intended to reprint *Remember Orr*. This they did successfully in June 1998. The evening after its launch in Belfast I attended a reception to mark Randalstown Historical Society's 1798 exhibition where I complained to Norman Scott of Randalstown about what I considered to be the many errors in *Remember Orr*. Norman, whose knowledge of the area few can match, remarked 'Ah, but you can't keep people away from Bigger!' By then I had determined to ignore '98 anniversary fever if it would allow the completion of a full account as possible of the Orrs. In presenting it now I am conscious that unforeseen material will immediately present itself but this is the time to draw a line under the Orrs and thank the many people who have helped me in my researches.

I first became aware of William Orr the watchmaker of Newgrove from James Kenny's book *As the Crow Flies over Rough Terrain*, but I had forgotten of this branch of the Orrs when Helen Rankin, then a fellow member of the Executive Committee of the Federation of Ulster Local Studies, passed on a letter from Australia asking for information on William Orr, watchmaker. While I eventually made the connection between this enquiry and James Kenny's account, my brain continued to make no real attempt to get into gear. Later, the Federation of Local History Societies organised a one-day seminar on Dublin records, to which they invited the Federation of Ulster Local Studies. That Saturday afternoon spent in the National Archives was tremendous. With its walls lined with indexes to the Rebellion Papers, Prisoners' Petitions and State of the Country Reports, I was sure that here was the place from which I could get beyond Bigger. At the close of the day, some of the less technophobic local historians were shown the new National Archive Internet web-site and the database of Irish men and women transported to Australia was demonstrated – Just type in a name and all the relevant entries would appear in a flash was the promise. Anyone got a name? Orr (my brain had suddenly clicked). Up came nine Orr records, the final one a petition from Antrim asking for the release of a William Orr, watchmaker.

There was only one thing to do and that was to try and make direct contact with Anne-Maree Whitaker in Australia, who had the first made inquiry relating to the watchmaker. Anne-Maree takes the credit for making the connection between this William Orr, Antrim and entries in a notebook held in the New South Wales State Archives simply referenced as *Diary of an Irish Rebel*. Dr Whitaker has been a tremendous help in providing other information on William Orr and the penal settlement of Botany Bay, which is described in her book on the United Irishmen transported to Australia, *Unfinished Revolution*. It is extremely unlikely that I would ever have found any of this by my own efforts. James Kenny has provided help on Newgrove, near Ballymena, and pointed me towards members of the Wilson family, formerly of Newgrove. Robert Wilson of Vancouver provided permission to reprint a series of documents on the Orr's of Creavery which he had in his possession. James Kenny has also granted permission to reprint some material he included in *As the Crow flies over Rough Terrain*.

Others pointed me on my way. Dr Brian Trainor's suggestion that I visit the India Office Library in London proved to be a very rewarding experience. Also in London, a librarian of the Guildhall Library, whose name I do not know, quickly unearthed books on early Australian shipwrecks. Robert Bonar, the recently retired Librarian of the Presbyterian Historical Society of Ireland helped access a ledger notebook which unravelled the Orr family links. Jim Rankin, a fellow member of the Antrim and District and Randalstown Historical Societies, generously provided me with references to James Orr which he had come across in the Public Record Office of Northern Ireland as well as newspaper references. Other historical society members, Francis Bateson, Frank Dale and Edmund McCann showed me places of '98 interest around Straffordstown and Duneane, while Maude McBride was able to fill in some of the Orr family history. Outside the bounds of the Society, Wilbert Crawford provided local information from Creavery as well as showing me the 'pike of William Orr' – which William Orr remains the question. Sammy Cameron took me to the 'Parade Field' in Groggan where the Rebels took their prisoners. David Campbell and Henry Cushnihan of Duneane and Norman Scott all provided information on William Orr's honeymoon in Duneane! John McCabe of Stoneyford guided me to the Home Office series of microfilms in PRONI and other Orr family material while Robert McClure provided a reference to Thomas Hamilton Jones. Local history feeds on coincidences and one such appeared when I realised that the farm now owned by my friend Harry Hume of Clogh was once owned by William Orr, the watchmaker. Subsequent trips with Harry to the Registry of Deeds in Dublin turned up more information on the Orrs.

I wish also to thank my colleagues Philip Elliot and Robert Rosell in the Department of Agriculture for Northern Ireland for their assistance with photography and fellow Historical Society member Katie Orme for her encouragement and editorial assistance, although all errors in the text remain my own responsibility.

As far as possible I have endeavoured to use original source material which has been included in the narrative or in the appendices. I have tried to maintain the original spelling, although as an amateur transcriber it is certain that I have unintentionally corrected some, including most instances where a letter f has been used instead of s, while adding my own imperfections. In many cases punctuation has been modified to incorporate full stops. I wish to acknowledge the permission of the following to reproduce material: The National Archives of Ireland, the Council of Trustees of the National Library of Ireland, The Board of Trinity College Dublin and the State Records of New South Wales.

On behalf of Antrim and District Historical Society and the Ulster Historical Foundation, I wish to express thanks for the financial support which this publication has received from the Enkalon Foundation, Antrim Borough Council, the Ulster Local History Trust Fund and the North Eastern Education and Library Board.

BOB FOY
14 OCTOBER 1999

Abbreviations

BNL	Belfast Newsletter
NLI	National Library of Ireland
PRONI	Public Record Office of Northern Ireland
Reg. of Deeds	Registry of Deeds, Dublin
SRNSW	State Records of New South Wales

NATIONAL ARCHIVES OF IRELAND

Reb. papers	Rebellion Papers
SPP	State prisoners petitions
PPC	Prisoner petitions and consultations
TCD	Library of Trinity College Dublin

ORIENTAL AND INDIA OFFICE COLLECTION, BRITISH LIBRARY

IOR	India Office Records
IOC	India Office Collection

PUBLIC RECORD OFFICE (KEW)

HO	Home Office documents
CO	Colonial Office documents

1
The vicissitudes
of their early days

M ost histories of the 1798 Rebellion in Ulster mention William Orr, for his execution on the 13th of October 1797 not only galvanised the United Irishmen of Ulster, but provided them with the rallying cry of *Remember Orr!* A farmer from the townland of Farranshane, near Antrim town, William Orr had been arrested in September 1796 and charged with illegally administering the United Irish oath to two soldiers, Hugh Wheatley and John Lindsay. For 200 years, his burial place in the Old Burying Ground of Templepatrick remained unmarked but, on the bicentenary of his death, a small memorial was erected in the graveyard. The driving force for this commemoration was the *Remember Orr Committee* which was formed by members of the Old Presbyterian Church of Templepatrick, a congregation of the Non-Subscribing Presbyterian Church in Ireland and a denomination with its roots in the New Light movement of Irish Presbyterianism.

William Orr was prominent on a local rather than a national scale in the Union of United Irishmen, but he belonged to a family which was at the heart of the revolutionary movement around Antrim. Almost one hundred years ago, Francis Joseph Bigger produced a biography of William Orr, entitled appropriately *Remember Orr*. However, many local historians who have used Bigger as a guide have found him to be an erratic source, his linking of William Orr to the New Light Presbyterian congregation in Antrim, being just one of a number of errors in his account. The purpose of this book is not simply to rake over the trail left by Bigger. Rather, using documents of the period, it seeks to shed light on the Antrim Orrs and their involvement in the events which convulsed Antrim during the summer of 1798 when Presbyterians rose to fight for the democratic ideals of liberty, equality and fraternity.[1]

In addition to William we find a brother, uncle and cousins who all suffered for their participation in the Rising of 1798. Of these, the story of his cousin and namesake is the most extraordinary and dramatic. Mentioned in passing by R.R. Madden in his memoirs of the United Irishmen, this William Orr has been distinguished as 'Rebel' Orr, as opposed to 'Remember' Orr, by James G. Kenny in his literary excursion through his own family's history.[2] While William 'Remember' Orr's grave had no headstone, the final resting place of William 'Rebel' Orr carries the following enigmatic epitaph.

> Here lies the remains of William Orr who, after various vicissitudes in early life, lived for many years at Newgrove where he died in the enjoyment of the peace of God.

This book relates the *vicissitudes* which afflicted all the Orrs.

CHAPTER 1 FOOTNOTES

1 Francis Joseph Bigger's *Remember Orr*. Published in 1906, a facsimile reprint was published in 1998, with a foreword by Kevin Whelan, by the Belfast Linenhall Library's United Irishmen Commemoration Committee. Bigger's book was the only one of a series entitled *The Northern Leaders of '98* to be printed.

2 Madden *Antrim and Down in '98*. pp. 50 & 56; Kenny (1988) *As the crow flies over rough terrain* p. 152.

2
In Widow William Orr's
I drank tea

Until the second half of this century, Antrim town was a fairly small affair; the population of around 2,000 in 1950 was more or less the same as it was in the 1790s. The town sits close to the north-eastern corner of Lough Neagh and, although the Lough plays little part in the town's economy, its presence ensures that the highways from Belfast and the south going to Derry in the west or northwards to Ballymena and Coleraine were funnelled through the town. As result, Antrim had its fair share of inns to cater for the needs of the traveller. The Six Mile Water flows through the town and it provided power for the mills on Mill Row, now the Riverside of Antrim. Fertile soils in the surrounding countryside gave the town a focus as a market for farm produce, although it was not farming which provided the livelihood of many living in the countryside, but the hand-loom weaving of linen. The weavers may not have been aware of it, but the last decade of the 18th century was close to the heyday of hand-loom weaving. The industry was still centred on the weaver working from his home and, with his wife and children spinning yarn, all the family could be put to work. Prices were high, buoyed up by the war with France but, within a generation, they would slump as production became automated in the new linen mills. Already the foundation of a new linen manufacturing aristocracy had been laid as some larger farmers invested in linen bleach greens.[1]

In an era of landlord and tenant, most farms around Antrim were owned by the Massereene family of Antrim Castle, one of the great land-owning families of Ulster. The Massereene family might have provided a strong social and political focus to the town, but in the 1790s the family was still afflicted by having the 2nd Earl at its head. Even by the standards of the class from which he was drawn, this Massereene's eccentricities approached insanity, which resulted in him spending a considerable part of his life in a French debtors' prison. His absence from the town had deprived it of a conservative political lead, similar to that provided by Lord Hillsborough in County Down, and the democratic tendencies of Presbyterians had been allowed to come to the fore, through enrolment in the Irish Volunteers of the 1780s and into local Freemason lodges. Massereene's neighbour to the west was a member of another great Irish landlord family, Lord O'Neill of Shane's Castle who had allied himself with the forces of reform in Irish politics. The O'Neill estates centred on Randalstown and extended westwards to the River Bann.[2]

The area around Antrim was solidly Presbyterian, as was the town where there were two Presbyterian churches: the Old Congregation and the Mill Row Congregation. The former was a 'New Light' or Non-Subscribing congregation and was the older of the two. The Old and New Light division of Irish Presbyterianism in the 1720s arose from the refusal of some 'New Light' Presbyterian ministers to subscribe to Presbyterian orthodoxy as prescribed in the Westminster Confession of Faith. This refusal led to their congregations being separated from the Synod of Ulster into the Non-Subscribing Presbytery of Antrim. The split could be traced to Antrim, where the Presbyterian minister in the town, John Abernethy, wrote an influential pamphlet entitled *Religious Obedience founded on Personal Persuasion* which crystallised much New Light thinking. Abernethy took his congregation into the new Presbytery of Antrim but not all members of the congregation were happy with their minister's doctrinal views and a minority formed a new and orthodox Presbyterian congregation in 1726. This had its meeting house in Mill Row, from which it took its name. Over the years this congregation prospered, relocating in 1836 to the present church building in Church Street. In the late 19th century it began to describe itself as First Antrim. In contrast, numbers attending the Old Congregation dwindled remorselessly in the 19th century and the congregation ceased to have a separate existence in the 1970s, when the remaining members came under the charge of the Old Congregation in Templepatrick.[3]

The minister of Mill Row in the 1790s was Alexander Montgomery, who apparently showed no tendency to dabble in radical politics. Robert Magill, who came from farming stock near Broughshane, succeeded him in 1820. Soon after Magill arrived in Antrim, the old dispute over Presbyterian orthodoxy in Ulster arose again. Magill became an enthusiastic lieutenant to Henry Cooke in the campaign which finally drove Unitarians out of the Synod of Ulster in 1827 to form the Non-Subscribing Presbyterian Church of Ireland. From his diary which he kept on a daily basis, it can be inferred that Magill was an energetic man with a deep interest in people. In his parish, he took the lead in promoting schools, collecting money for the Mendicity Society of Antrim, which provided for the poor, and was active in medical matters. Indeed, Magill's diary portrays him as the would-be doctor, for he was meticulous in recording the ailments afflicting his parishioners and kept records as to causes of death. He personally undertook the inoculation of children with cow-pox to protect them against the dis-figuring and deadly small-pox. Above all he was punctilious in visiting the members of his congregation on a regular basis. On the 31 July 1827 he visited families living in a group of townlands about two miles north-east of Antrim. The entry for that day is as follows:

> 31 July 1827. Visited the families of Widow Moore, Mary Johnson, Mrs James Finlay, Thomas Anderson, John Orr, Widow John Orr, Anthony Roy, Adam Linn, Samuel Steel, David McQuillan, Widow Samuel Orr, Widow William Orr, William Kirkpatrick, Widow Kearney, Robert French, James Campbell, John Kirkpatrick, Robert Carson, William Groves, Widow Greenlees, John Crawford and Alexander Black.
> Baptized John Carson, son of the above named Robert Carson. He was born yesterday – dined in John Campbell's and drank tea there – also in Widow William Orr's I drank tea. Visited old Mr Reford.[4]

The Orrs whom Magill visited were related to William 'Remember' Orr, not the least of whom was William's wife Isabella, the 'Widow William Orr' with whom he 'drank tea'. Magill's visit may qualify only as an historical curiosity but it is for another of his interests, namely family history, that he is important in the story of the Orrs for he used his visits to unravel the genealogical links between the families of his congregation. The resulting family trees were meticulously entered in a ledger book which he entitled *Names of seat-holders and their families and also names etc. of such individuals as belong to the [Mill Row] congregation but have no seat. Extracted from the records of the parish and other documents by the Revd. Robert Magill.* This lists families, their pew numbers arranged in a running order to facilitate the minister's visits, and records their burial place. Four Orr families, each shown to be related to the other, are listed as having their burial ground at Templepatrick, about five miles from Antrim.

Before examining these four families, it is clear from their inclusion in Magill's volume that they were all members of the Mill Row Congregation in Antrim. Indeed, the denominational links which can be established for the Orrs are all with Orthodox or Covenanting Presbyterian ministers. Scribbled side-notes to Magill's *Names of seat-holders* show that Orrs were baptized by John Rankin who was the Mill Row minister from 1751 to 1789. Rankin's successor, Alexander Montgomery was an executor to the will made by William Orr shortly before his execution. At his execution, Orr was attended by two ministers of the Old Light persuasion: William Stavely a Covenanting minister and Adam Hill, the Presbyterian minister of Ballynure. It is simply not credible to place William Orr, as Francis Bigger does, in the New Light congregation of Antrim. Bigger wrote his account at the turn of the last century and exactly how he came by his information is unclear but his book is full of erratic assertions. Certainly he cannot have consulted either the records of the Old Congregation, which is surprising as he knew the then minister W.S. Smith, or Thomas West, who was then minister of Mill Row. In contrast to Bigger, Magill must be considered a most reliable source with regard to the Orr genealogy. In addition to having used church records, which are now destroyed, Magill's diary shows him to have been in friendly and sociable contact with many of the Orr families, as evidenced by the drinking of tea with Widow William Orr.[5]

The Orrs of Kilbegs and Farranshane
The Orr home farm was at Kilbegs, a townland some two miles from Antrim and not far from Lord O'Neill's demesne of Shane's Castle. Kilbegs includes part of the Milltown, a hamlet created by Lord O'Neill around the corn-mill there, when he moved the ancient village of Eden-duff-

carrick which was considered to be too close O'Neill's residence in the old castle. The townland is quite flat and a racecourse was located behind the Orr farm. Magill records that three Samuel Orrs, the first of whom died in 1767, headed the household at Kilbegs for three consecutive generations. This first Samuel married Agnes Micheal or Mitchel and they had five sons: William, James, John, Samuel and Joseph. William died young while Joseph went to England, leaving James, John and Samuel to form three distinct Orr family lines around Antrim. James farmed at Creavery, John at The Folly on the outskirts of Antrim while Samuel continued on in his father's house at Kilbegs.[6]

This second Samuel Orr married Alice and was the father to three sons: William 'Remember' Orr, James and Samuel, and four daughters: Nancy, Sarah, Eliza and Jane. From William and James, two more Orr branches were founded. James moved to Cranfield, on the other side of Randalstown, where he married a Miss Mulligan, an heiress who brought to the marriage property at Cranfield, close to the shores of Lough Neagh. He alone of the three brothers appears not to have played a role in the United Irishmen. Indeed from 1791 he was High Constable for the Barony of Upper Toome and so was involved in law enforcement and the collection of the county cess under the authority of the County Antrim Grand Jury. William, the eldest son, inherited land at Toome and Farranshane, which his father had acquired for £800 in 1779 and where, according to Bigger, William operated a bleach green. He married Isabella Greer from the Parish of Duneane, about six miles west of Randalstown in 1788 and the couple began to raise a family at Farranshane.[7]

Samuel was the youngest of the three brothers, but it was he who took over the farm at Kilbegs on the death of his father in 1796. Magill records that Church of Ireland curates married both Samuel and William 'Remember' Orr: William by Rev. McClusky of Duneane and Samuel by Rev. Wright of Donegore. Samuel Orr was only 18 years of age in 1792 when he married Mary Redmond who was 13 years his senior. Mary was probably a member of the Redmond family of Thornhill in the townland of Lisnevenagh, about four miles north of Antrim. The preference of the Redmonds, Orrs and Greers for Church of Ireland weddings reflects their wealth rather than membership of that denomination. Until the 1840s, marriages conducted by Presbyterian clergymen in Ireland had an ambivalent status in Irish law which specifically recognised only marriages conducted by Church of Ireland and Roman Catholic clergymen. This raised the possibility that children of Presbyterian marriages could be

Kilbegs. The former home of the Orrs of Antrim.

regarded as illegitimate in law, with attendant problems in property inheritance. This uncertainty led many prosperous Presbyterian families such as the Orrs, Greers and Redmonds to resort to Church of Ireland marriages while maintaining their day-to-day adherence to the Presbyterian church.[8]

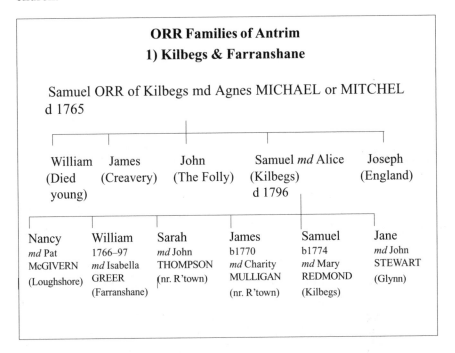

ORR Families of Antrim
1) Kilbegs & Farranshane

Samuel ORR of Kilbegs md Agnes MICHAEL or MITCHEL d 1765

| William (Died young) | James (Creavery) | John (The Folly) | Samuel *md* Alice (Kilbegs) d 1796 | Joseph (England) |

| Nancy *md* Pat McGIVERN (Loughshore) | William 1766–97 *md* Isabella GREER (Farranshane) | Sarah *md* John THOMPSON (nr. R'town) | James b1770 *md* Charity MULLIGAN (nr. R'town) | Samuel b1774 *md* Mary REDMOND (Kilbegs) | Jane *md* John STEWART (Glynn) |

The Orrs of Creavery

The townland of Creavery is about three miles from Kilbegs and is north of Antrim. At present it touches the main road to Ballymena at the Ramble Inn but in 1798 the main coach road to Ballymena ran through Creavery along what is now called the Thornhill Road. The Creavery branch of the family was started by James Orr, who was a brother of the second Samuel Orr of Kilbegs. One year after Samuel's death in 1796, James was also dead. He had married Eliza Orr and Magill records five children; two daughters and three sons: John, Robert and William 'Rebel' Orr. This William was born in 1774 and he was, therefore, some eight years younger than his cousin and namesake at Farranshane. William trained as a watchmaker in Dublin while his elder brother, John Orr, continued to farm at Creavery but John also had a blacksmith's shop in Creavery. As will be seen, John and William were each implicated in the United Irishmen and both suffered for their involvement but nothing is known of the remaining brother Robert. Their two sisters each married: Nancy to John Johnson of Ballydonnan in the Ards and Eliza to James Hughes of Magherafelt.

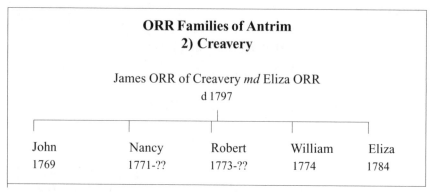

ORR Families of Antrim
2) Creavery

James ORR of Creavery *md* Eliza ORR
d 1797

John	Nancy	Robert	William	Eliza
1769	1771-??	1773-??	1774	1784

The Orrs of The Folly

Today, The Folly in Antrim finds expression as residential district in the suburbs of the town, but in 1798 it was a farm about a mile from the outskirts of the town. It was here that John Orr resided at the foot of a tree-lined lane in the townland of Bleerick, although in a property deed he is described as a mason rather than a farmer. After the deaths of his brothers, Samuel at Kilbegs in 1796 and James at Creavery in 1797, John Orr was left as the only surviving son of the first Samuel Orr of Kilbegs and was the most senior member of the Orr clan around Antrim. As such he was an uncle to William Orr of Farranshane, Samuel Orr at Kilbegs and John Orr and William Orr at Creavery. Like each of them he was deeply involved with the United Irishmen and was one of the few County Antrim names to appear in the *Black Book of the Rebellion*, which lists United Irishmen, mostly from County Down.[9]

John was married to Fanny Carson of Killead and they had three children, Peggy, Samuel and James. Of these, Samuel was married by 1798 and was farming at Harp Hall, in the townland of Hurtletoot, directly behind the farm of his cousin, William Orr, in Farranshane. This Samuel died fairly young in 1807 and it was his wife, Ellen Harper, who was the 'Widow Samuel Orr' that Mr Magill visited in 1827.[10]

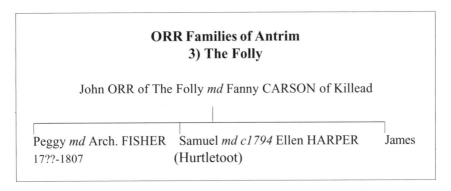

ORR Families of Antrim
3) The Folly

John ORR of The Folly *md* Fanny CARSON of Killead

Peggy *md* Arch. FISHER   Samuel *md c1794* Ellen HARPER   James
17??-1807   (Hurtletoot)

Other United links can be established from Magill's family trees. Nancy, the sister of Samuel Orr of Kilbegs and of William Orr of Farranshane, was married to Pat McGivern of the Loughshore to the south of Antrim beside Lough Neagh and approximately in the townland of Corbally. McGivern is an uncommon name around Antrim and has now died out in the Loughshore. In the accounts of the Battle of Antrim a James McGivern

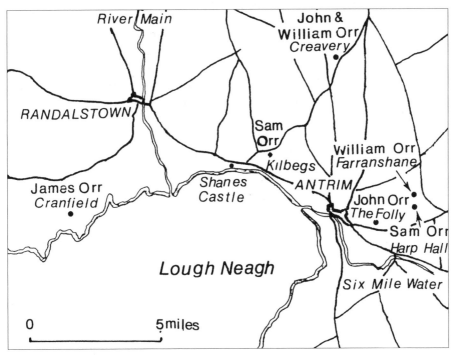

The Orrs of Antrim in the late 1790s. The road system is taken from the 1808 edition of Lendrick's map of County Antrim.

is recorded as volunteering to lead a United Irish attack on the Castle garden walls and he was one of the leaders proclaimed in July 1798. Another sister, Jane was married to John Stewart of Glynn who, in the *Black Book of the Rebellion*, is listed as a United Irish leader in County Antrim and is specifically noted as a brother-in-law of William Orr.[11]

In total, there were five Orr families living around Antrim in the late 1790s at Kilbegs, Creavery, The Folly, Farranshane and Hurtletoot. Together they formed an arc of United Irish influence around the town. The Orrs were all comfortably set up, indeed one might suspect that, for some of the younger generation, their relative prosperity had come too easily. For example at Kilbegs, Samuel Orr at the age of 25 found himself in charge of a large farm. They were representative of a numerous and growing class in County Antrim, for whom the second half of the eighteenth century had not been unkind in terms of accumulating material wealth. They would have been keenly aware that their growing economic power was accompanied by a diminishing political influence. In 1790 Antrim town had a fairly extensive electorate of around 300 for parliamentary elections, which included the male heads of most households. By 1795 this was reduced to 30 whose support for Massereene was so certain that the election of the two Antrim seats was not even contested. Contrary to the expectations of the 1780s when the Irish Parliament had won legislative independence, power in the 1790s had become even more entrenched in the hands of a tiny and almost exclusively Church of Ireland political elite. For all of the Orrs, righting this wrong was to prove very costly.[12]

CHAPTER 2 FOOTNOTES

1 For histories and descriptions of Antrim town see (i) Smyth (1984) and (ii) the Ordnance Survey Memoir of the town in 1838 (Day & McWilliams, 1995).

2 For the career of the 2nd Earl see Malcomson (1972).

3 Hughes (1996) *Hewn from the rock* is a comprehensive history of Mill Row/First Antrim. An article by the Rev. John Nelson, written as an introduction to Smith (1996) *Memories of '98,* provides some information on the declining strength of the Old Congregation in Antrim.

4 The diary for 1826 and 1827 is reprinted in full in Kenny's *As the crow flies over rough terrain* from which this entry is taken.

5 Magill's *Names of seat-holders* is now in the keeping of the Presbyterian Historical Society of Ireland. A microfilm copy is in PRONI. Stewart (1995) in *Summer soldiers* refers to William Orr as a 'New Light Presbyterian' (p. 49). However the assertion that this was not the case is hardly a new one. The Ordnance Survey Memoir noted that Widow Orr was a member of the 'Orthodox' Mill Row congregation in Antrim (Day & MacWilliams, *op cit.*, p7). Smyth (1984) also mentions William Orr's family membership of Mill Row. In his 1935 history of the congregation, Matthew Majury, who was then the minister there, refers to William Orr 'of Glorious Memory'. Majury's predecessor was Thomas West who was installed in 1867. In his 1902 history of the congregation, he refers to *Magill's Names of seat-holders* and the inclusion there of William Orr. As a young minister, West visited the youngest daughter of William Orr at Farranshane, writing of her: 'I remember Wilhelmina Moorehead. She was at communion in 1868. I visited her during her last illness and attended her funeral.' West was a determined opponent of Irish Home Rule and controversially opened his church for the signing of the Ulster Covenant in 1912. One wonders if his political opinions played a part in the lack of any communication with Bigger, who was a passionate advocate for Home Rule.

6 The date of the first Samuel Orr's death is taken from the list of Orr wills given in the Down & Connor Will book in PRONI. A racecourse at Kilbegs is marked on the 1780 Lendrick map for County Antrim (PRONI D/1062/22/4).

7 References to James Orr's career as a Constable can be found in the County Antrim Grand Jury Upper and Lower Toome Grant Warrant Book 1791-1804 (PRONI ANT/4/2/7/1) and *Belfast Newsletter* 5 April 1799. Jim Rankin first noted the references to James Orr in the Grand Jury records while Norman Scott provided information on the marriage of James Orr. Samuel Orr's purchase of Farranshane in Reg. of Deeds 331/118/221029 & 314/360/218412.

8 Magill also gives a brief family tree of Isabella Orr's parents.

9 Description of John Orr as a mason is in a deed for the farm at Hurtletoot (Reg. of Deeds 517/245/339661). John Orr was one of only a handful of mid-Antrim men listed in the Black Book of the Rebellion (PRONI D/272/1).

10 Bigger was apparently unaware of the existence of the Orrs of The Folly and persistently confused Sam Orr of Hurtletoot with his cousin Sam Orr of Kilbegs.

11 For reference to McGivern see M'Skimmon p.123. The entry for Jane's husband is as follows 'James Stewart of Glynn P[rovincal committee member] Brother in law to Orr that was executed and lives near where the Revd. Mr Maine lives and has his living' (PRONI D/272/1).

12 Smyth (1985) p. 38 gives details of Antrim elections and electorate.

3
Was Billy McKeever
the man?

The path of the United Irishmen led from an advocacy of radical reform to one of sweeping away the old order – a revolution – but a revolt against Dublin Castle would bring them into direct conflict with the Crown forces. This was too daunting a prospect for many of the leaders who considered that their only realistic hope of success depended on the arrival of a French army of liberation. Nonetheless they sought to undermine the Government by inducing individual soldiers to become United Irishmen so that, when the rising came, Dublin Castle would be faced, not only by the mass of the people and the French, but also by a military mutiny. Facing this unpleasant prospect and having to fight a war against Revolutionary France in Europe, the West Indies, Africa and Asia, the Government began to contemplate ever more drastic measures to contain the rising tide of sedition in Ireland. New laws extended the boundaries of repression with the 1796 Insurrection Act ordering the death penalty for those who administered the United Irish oath.

On the 24th April 1796 two soldiers, Hugh Wheatley and John Lindsay, stopped in the town of Antrim on their way to re-join their regiment in Derry. Both belonged to the Fifeshire Fencible Regiment, one of the Scottish regiments drafted into Ireland to bolster the Crown forces. Wheatley was a lance-corporal while Lindsay was a private. The two men found accommodation in the town, Lindsay in John Hyndman's Swan Inn. Hyndman was a United man, perhaps prominent in the organisation, but, as will be seen, sufficiently prudent as to avoid getting himself caught. He soon began to press the two men to come over to the Brotherhood of Affection, quoting to them Scripture in support of brotherly love and union. In the evening Wheatley and Lindsay fell in with John Orr of Creavery, who invited them for a drink with him and his friends. As the evening wore on, the conversation turned to matters political and the soldiers were asked how they rated their situation. Their lives were surely not worth a farthing to their commanders, and would not life be better if they had a shilling a day, rather than sixpence? By the time the evening was finished, John Orr had individually induced the two to swear to be true to the United Irishmen and to keep their secrets. The subsequent assertion by the two soldiers that they were drunk by this time may have had some basis to it. After they were sworn, others instructed them in the secret signs of the United Irishmen.

The next day the two soldiers lingered on in Antrim, perhaps encouraged that their landlord had shown no indication of wanting any payment for their accommodation. In the evening another night of free drinking began. Their companions boasted of the numbers of soldiers they had already recruited, who would rise up at 'a moment's warning'. A baker from the town produced the printed Constitution or Rule Book of the United Irishmen. Another man present was James Campbell, a neighbour of William Orr at Farranshane, who returned to Hyndman's inn the next morning and invited the soldiers to come to his house that evening. Here they were entertained with meat and drink and Campbell was sufficiently confident (and/or drunk) to show them the arms he had in his own house. Matters, according to Campbell, were so far gone that it would be impossible to stop them. Taking some air, he showed his visitors the draw-well in his garden and jocularly suggested it would be a good place to throw the aristocracy into. At the close of another heavy evening Campbell had promised the soldiers that he would divide a farm of land between them when the Government was 'overturned'.

On the fourth day of their visit to Antrim, the soldiers went for a walk with Hyndman, who presumably wanted to keep an eye on them. That evening they met another man in the inn, whom they understood was also called Campbell. This was hardly a chance encounter, for this Campbell was Billy McKeever, a prominent United Irish leader from Upperlands in South Derry. McKeever suggested they should go back to James Campbell's house, who again obligingly treated them with 'meat and drink'. After more chat 'on the subject of the United Irishmen', Campbell took his visitors to find William Orr, who was located in a field sowing flax. Others were gathered up, including McKeever/Campbell, and the party went to William Orr's house where a committee meeting of United Irishmen took place. The two soldiers had been given the choice of deserting, in which case, they would want for neither money nor clothing, or continuing in the army but recruiting a United Society from the Fifeshire Fencibles. They took the latter option and Wheatley, the most senior of the two, was entrusted with a copy of the Constitution Book of the United Irishmen and given five shillings. Before this, William Orr had insisted that Wheatley swear another oath to be true to the United Irishmen and keep their secrets. Prior to the soldiers' departure, McKeever gave them six and a half pennies and a message to a Mr Orr, a copper-smith in Derry.[1]

Wheatley and Lindsay proceeded on to Derry, where they made no attempt to reveal the nature of their stay in Antrim to their officers and there is evidence that they became known as sympathisers to United elements in the city. Within weeks however, Billy McKeever, alias Campbell had been arrested and lodged in Derry Jail. The agent for his arrest was the Rev. Clotworthy Soden, a magistrate from Maghera who, at the same time, had got wind of the two Fencibles' activities in Antrim. At the end of May, Soden sent a letter to James Durham, Colonel of the Fifeshire Fencibles, who summonsed Wheatley and Lindsay. Facing a probable court martial for allowing themselves to be sworn, the two promptly confessed all. Their subsequent statements emphasise the influence of drink in the affair and unspecified threats made to force them to be sworn as United Irishmen. Soden's intention was to get evidence to convict McKeever, but neither of the two soldiers was aware of McKeever's alias as Campbell. This is evident from the summary of their statement which Durham sent to Soden and reproduced here.

The statement makes clear that the two soldiers were unsure of the identity of either John or William Orr. John Orr is distinguished only as the shorter of the two, and William as a taller, stouter man. It was Durham who made the connection between one of the Campbells the soldiers had met and McKeever and his letter marks references to this man as

Campbell+. At the end of the letter, Durham writes 'Where you see Campbell marked thus +, Billy McKeever was the man'. The presence of McKeever at the Farranshane meeting agrees with James Hope's assertion that it was William McKeever who swore the two soldiers.

LONDONDERRY MAY 29TH 1796. A COPY   *REB. PAPERS 620/23/129*

LETTER TO CLOTWORTHY SODEN, MAGHERA

FROM JAMES DURHAM COL FIFE FENCIBLES

Sir

Upon receipt of yours I immediately confined Wheatley and Lindsay and this day had them examined before Mr Lecky & Alderman Kennedy and Langford Heyland Esq. who happened to be in Derry. The men upon being sent for offer'd to tell all that had pafsed during the four days they were in Antrim, the heads of which I send you. They were coming from Scotland to Derry and were billeted upon one Hyndman who keeps the sign of the Swan in Antrim, That in the evening some country people and towns-people asked them to drink and treated them with liqueur until they were drunk and that there were four men of the party, two of them by the name of Campbell+ and two by name Orr, That these men represented to them how ill they were used as soldiers & how ill they were paid and offered them one shilling a day if they would take the oath to the United Irishmen and that they would soon be Captains, That they were threatened to murder if they did not, That one of the men of the name Orr, the shortest of the two, did administer an oath to them one by one in a room by themselves, That next day they took them out to Campbell's, a mile and a half from Antrim, where he promised to divide a farm with them when they had overthrown the Constitution. Campbell+ then carried them to Orr's house, not the one who swore them, a taller stouter man. There was a Committee of ten members and Orr, who swore them again, and who delivered to them a book, call'd the Constitution. Which book they swore to conceal and to get in as many men to swear upon as they could, that in Hyndman's house they were taught all the signs and counter signs, that Hyndman was more active and pressing with them to take the oath than any of the party, That they were told many of the Dublin Militia in Coleraine had taken this oath and almost all the Limerick. That they were even now making great progress amongst the Fleet and had secured so many in the Fort of Charlemont that it would be given up to them, whenever they chose to rise, that powder came to Belfast from America in flax seed casks, that they were offer'd cloths to desert in and upon coming away Campbell+, who is now in Derry Gaol, gave them a letter to Mr Orr coppersmith in Derry, that they sent people to go with them beyond Randalstown, that as soon as they were left to themselves, they burned the book, that almost every person in Antrim and Randalstown knew the countersigns and that the Billet Masters in both places were sworn, that they knew no-body by the name of Billy McKeever as you mention, a few hours before your letter came to me, a man came to Wheatley in the street and informed him he would be taken up and bid him be sure and deny all. I have now given you the heads of their examination which the magistrates will send you at full length. My Regt. marches to Belfast on Monday the 30th, these two will be in Antrim on Thursday or Friday. I think Orr and Hyndman ought to be taken up. I have the honor to be Sir

JAMES DURHAM   COL. FIFE FENCIBLES.

PS It was the opinion of the magistrates here that these men might be of more use when at liberty, than when confined, they halt at Randalstown on Thursday. Where you see Campbell marked thus + , Billy McKeever was the man.

However, although the soldiers' statement refers to Campbell/McKeever, there is nothing in it to suggest that it was McKeever who swore them, although he comes over as one who ordered them around. Indeed if it had been McKeever who had done the deed, which was a capital offence, their evidence would have surely been used to prosecute McKeever as he was already in custody.[2]

When Durham heard his soldiers' story he was keen that Hyndman and Orr would be arrested and he wanted the Magistrates in Antrim to take a statement from the two soldiers. The Fifeshire regiment was to move to Belfast and Durham proposed to make them available as they passed through Antrim. Accordingly early in June, a joint statement was taken by the Rev. George Macartney, the vicar of Antrim, from Wheatley and Lindsay. For some reason, another duplicate statement had to be taken by Macartney in mid-July, on the instruction of Judge Chamberlain who was one of the judges who sat at the Carrickfergus assizes.[3] Only the second of the two survives in the Rebellion Papers in Dublin and a transcript is reproduced here. The original is in Macartney's handwriting and it is Macartney whom we must suppose added the detail identifying the Orrs. John Orr, identified in the Derry statement only as the shorter of the two is given as John Orr, son of James Orr of Creavery, farmer; presumably to distinguish him from another Orr family which was then resident in Creavery.[4] The taller and stouter Orr is clearly identified by Macartney as William Orr of Farranshane, farmer. Otherwise the statement Macartney took was quite consistent with the one the soldiers had made in Derry, although each contains minor details not mentioned in the other. There is little to suppose that the second was intentionally embellished by the soldiers, except in their desire to emphasise that they were unwilling participants. Both statements mention that John Orr swore the soldiers during the first night they were in Antrim but that William Orr issued a Constitution Book of the United Irishmen. Macartney seemed keen to note that Hyndman, although considered by the soldiers to have been at the centre of their recruitment, had not at any time swore the two soldiers. That both John Orr and William Orr had done so, put them in breach of the Insurrection Act.

COUNTY OF ANTRIM   *REB. PAPERS 620/24/41* [5]

The examination of Hugh Wheatley, Lance Corporal and John Lindsay, a private soldier in his Majesties' Fife Shire Fencible Regiment, who being duely sworn on the Holy Evangelists and examined on oath, say that on or about the twenty fourth of April last, being in the Town of Antrim in said County on their way to their regiment at that time quartered in the City of Londonderry and John Lindsay being billeted in the house of John Hyndman, innkeeper.

Hugh Wheatley for himself saith that, he having call'd at the house of Hyndman to see his comrade John Lindsay, a person, who he is informed and believes is John Orr, son of James Orr of Creavery, farmer, followed him into *the* house and asked examinant to drink with him there, which examinant accordingly did; And that after examinant and Orr had drank for some time, several other persons came into their company (all of whom examinant has reason to believe were United Irishmen) and that Orr and *the* other persons asked examinant and Lindsay how they liked their kind of life (meaning the life of a soldier) and also if they cou'd not live better on a shilling than six pence a day. And said at same time that examinant's life and Lindsay's life was not worth a farthing unless they came into their way of life (meaning as examinant believes the life of United Irishmen);

And examinant further saith that the other persons having gone by degrees out of the room that, John Orr tender'd a book to examinant and compelled him to swear to be true to the United Irishmen and keep their secrets or words to that effect, and that before examinant took *this* oath,

Orr told examinant that he and examinant Lindsay shou'd get some places of profit in *the* Society of United Irishmen. And John Lindsay for himself saith that soon after he had heard that Hugh Wheatley had be sworn, John Orr took examinant into another room in house and having put a book into examinant's hand swore him to be true to United Irishmen and keep their secrets, which oath was so taken in presence of a person unknown to examinant.

And examinant Hugh Wheatley for himself saith that, at the time that he believes Orr was so swearing, three or four persons who were of the company of Orr came into room where examinant was sitting and made use of several signs which they taught examinant and told him they were the signs of the United Irishmen and told examinant that the intention of United Irishmen was to make a reform of parliament and that if they did not get that by fair means they intended to rise up against Government and overturn the Constitution of the Kingdom.

Examinant further saith that in the evening of next day, a person whose name examinant is informed and believes is James Campbell of the Sixteen Towns of Antrim, who resides about two miles from Antrim, came to examinant in the house of Hyndman; And Hyndman and others who were drinking in the examinant's house, told examinant what a fine thing it was to be United Irishmen, on which a person unknown to examinant, who examinant is informed resides in Antrim and is a baker by trade, brought a book out of his pocket which he and the others called their Constitution, a part of which he read and which examinant understood to be intended to overturn the present Government of this Kingdom; And these said persons stated to examinants the number of men they had ready in a moment's warning to effect the same and they had got a sufficient number of military ready at Charlemont to secure that fort and examinants say that they continued with *these* persons till about eleven o'clock that night; And that about nine o'clock next morning James Campbell and two or three other persons who were with examinant the night before, returned to said house, when Campbell insisted that examinants should come to his house in the evening of that day, which they accordingly did;

And at Campbell's house, James Campbell entertained examinants with meat and drink and Campbell often declared in conversation that night that they (meaning the United Irishmen) had carried matters so far as it would be impossible to stop them and at the same time shewed examinants different kinds of arms which he had in his house; And examinants further say that Campbell shewed them a draw well which well is at present at the front of his house, which James Campbell said would be nice place to put aristocrats and aristocracy into; And

Campbell immediately after took examinants into his garden and shewed them a book of the same kind they had seen before called the Constitution Book of said United Irishmen and informs examinant that he, John Campbell, had different farms and that, after matters were brought to a proper crisis (meaning thereby as Examinants believe when the present Government should be overturned), that he would divide said farms between examinants and that they returned that night to house of Hyndman in Antrim.

And examinants further say that on the next day, after having been walking in the country with Hyndman, they returned to the house of Hyndman in the evening, where the examinants met James Campbell and another person of that name who (examinants are informed) is in Derry Jail, who insisted that examinants should go again to house of John Campbell; Which examinants did, and after being some time in house and being entertained by Campbell with meat and drink and conversing on the subject of United Irishmen, that Campbell took examinants into a field where they found a man whose name (examinants are informed and believe) is William Orr of Farinshane in said County, farmer, who was sowing flax seed; And who immediately assembled a number of persons, whom deponents believe to have been a committee of United Irishmen, and that John Campbell went with examinants and said persons into the house of William Orr at Farinshane and on their way there that they met the other Campbell (who examinants hear is in Derry Jail);[6]

And that John Campbell and the other Campbell and examinants having gone into the house of William Orr, Orr put a book into the hand of Hugh Wheatley and desired him to swear that he would be true to United Irishmen and keep their secrets and he would not for any reward or fear of being punished give information against them; Which oath examinant at first declined taking but by being threatened by said Orr and his party, of which John Campbell was one, that examinant was forced in their presence to take oath; And Orr at same time swore examinant in the presence of the John Campbell and of the above party in his house to take care of the Constitution Book which he gave him and gave examinant five English shillings and that Campbell, now in Derry Jail, gave examinant six pence half penny and told examinant that the United Irishmen had got gunpowder over from America in hogsheads which passed as flaxseed;

And both examinants say that they paid nothing for the meat and drink they got in Hyndman's house during the time they were in Antrim but believed was paid by the United Irishmen. Hyndman having told them that they were not to pay anything and that if they wanted money they should not want it, and examinants farther say that Hyndman pressed

them to become United Irishmen shortly after coming to his house and quoted several passages of scripture to them exciting brotherly love and union, but that (notwithstanding his having used very persuasion to accomplish his purposes and his being instrumental in bringing John Orr to them who swore examinants in his house as above) he, Hyndman, was not present when examinants were sworn by either of the Orrs.
Examinants farther say that John Campbell told them that if they would leave the Army they should want for neither money or cloathes.
John Lindsay saith that he saw William Orr administer above oath to examinant Hugh Wheatley.

Sworn 17th July 1796 before me.
   GEO. MACARTNEY
   JOHN LINDSAY
   HUGH WHEATLEY

Sworn before me by permission of Mr Justice Chamberlaine the 17th day of July 1796, the original deposition taken by me in the beginning of June last having not been yet sent to the assizes by the Attorney General. Examinants bound to prosecute from assizes to assizes till above persons are tried for the above offences in the sum of £30 each.

   GEO. MACARTNEY

Three months elapsed after the first statement of Wheatley and Lindsay before an arrest was made. During this time William Orr kept out of sight and it can be assumed that his cousin John Orr adopted a similar strategy. There is a tradition that, when soldiers arrived at a house in Glenwherry in the Antrim hills, where William Orr was hiding, he only escaped capture by fleeing into the mist covered moors. However by September 1796, his father, 'old Sam Orr' of Kilbegs, was dying and this led William to risk a final visit to his father. In Antrim, Kirke, who was probably in charge of the military detachment there, heard of the seriousness of Sam Orr's condition and surmised that William would wish to visit his father before he died. On the night of the 14 September, he led a party of twenty one soldiers out to Kilbegs where he found his quarry hiding in 'a press in the wall'. William Orr was promptly arrested, but, rather than returning to Antrim with their prize, the soldiers rode on to Creavery in the hope of arresting John Orr and also to James Campbell's home but neither John Orr nor James Campbell was be found. This description of the arrest comes from the letter, reproduced here, sent by Robert Macartney to his father the Rev. Macartney who was in England.

Having arrested Orr, the soldiers required authorisation to commit him to prison and, in the absence of the Rev. Macartney, the soldiers went the following morning to another magistrate, Jackson Clarke, to get a committal. Clarke lived outside Antrim, at the Steeple, almost beside Farranshane, but he refused to accept the statement that Macartney had obtained from Wheatley and Lindsay as sufficient evidence to justify Orr's committal. Alarmed by the prospect of Orr being released, John Staples set off at 10 o'clock in the morning for Lisburn where he was fortunate enough to meet Lord Castlereagh who signed a warrant consigning Orr to Carrickfergus Gaol, with an additional instruction that the gaoler should prevent anyone, other than a magistrate, making contact with William Orr. Staples hurried back to Antrim, which he only reached in the late afternoon at 5 pm where there was a 'great mob'. Fearing an attempt might be made to rescue Orr, preparations were made to move him immediately to Carrickfergus and so, at 6 pm, William Orr left Antrim for the last time escorted by twenty soldiers.

SEPT. 1796, SAT   *REB. PAPERS 620/25/132*

Dear Father

It is with infinite pleasure I sit down to write to you, as I think that affairs here wear a much better prospect than they have done. Old Sam Orr has been dying this week past. Kirke suspected that his son William might have returned to his father before he died – On these grounds he went out last night with Beard and twenty men and surrounded the house and got Orr hid in a press in the wall; they then went out in search of Campbell & John Orr but without success.

Clarke refused giving a committal on your examination & Stables [sic] went off at ten this morning to Lisburn to have fresh depositions taken, but luckily at Lisburn met Lord Castlereagh, who immediately gave him a committal upon your examinations & wrote particular directions to the jailer to keep him from conversation with anyone except himself, to wit the jailer or some magistrate. Stables came home at five & Orr was taken off with 20 Dragoons at six, There was a great mob.

Sam Neilson, Capt. Russell, Haslett, Jno. Young, Robt Osborne, one Shanaghan an attorney's clerk & Kennedy the head composer for the Northern Star were all taken up in Belfast yesterday for high treason. Chas Teeling & an apothecary in Lisburn were also taken up & Fitzgerald who keeps a store house at Sandy Bay was taken up by a troop of the 22nd from Lisburn. There is the greatest consternation here.

While Stables was at Lisburn there were three parties went out in pursuit of other men, Lord Castlereagh was to go to Col Durham & have Wheatley and Lindsay secured; he kept your deposition to take a copy of them.

I think Clarkes refusing to commit Orr & also refusing to detain a man from Magherafelt who damned the King and with whom papers were found by which it appeared that he had fled for fear of being taken up, ought to be taken notice of.

As[?] You[?] will be very inquisitive I think it right to make this a double letter. The corn is all down except the piece [sic] in the race field at the gap. We have no better news from what I have mentioned. All here join in love to you.

Your ever affectionate son,
  R. MACARTNEY.

We got yours this morning. They took Orr this evening as apprehensions were entertained of a rescue of which had it taken place, Clarke would have been the cause.

My Mother and Aunt wish you to write to Sally & make her write to us here. My mother approves of you prolonging your stay.[7]

As Macartney's letter makes clear, other United leaders in Antrim and Down were arrested at the same time, including Samuel Neilson and Henry Joy McCracken in Belfast. These men were taken to Kilmainham jail in Dublin but Orr remained in Carrickfergus, as there was evidence against him which would support a trial. Despite these setbacks, the United Irishmen in the North attempted to turn the arrests to propaganda purposes. Orr's absence from home during the summer of 1796 would have been at the expense of his farm with an added complication that his wife, Isabella, gave birth to their fifth child, also called Isabella, some seven weeks before her husband's arrest. After the arrest, United men twice assembled in their hundreds under the guise of 'neighbours' to save William Orr's crop of corn and to gather in his potatoes. These 'hasty diggings', sometimes involving thousands of diggers, were so called for the short time required to bring the crop in and demonstrated not only solidarity with their imprisoned comrade but also the strength and organisational discipline of the United Irishmen. The United Irishmen's Belfast newspaper, the *Northern Star*, reported approvingly a rash of similar events in Antrim and Down during the autumn of 1796 but in November they were prohibited.[8]

What sort of a man was William Orr? Two contrasting descriptions of him have survived. The first, and a flattering one, appeared in *The Press*, the United Irishmen's newspaper in Dublin and was based on a visit to Orr while he was being held in Carrickfergus gaol during 1797. As such it may have been penned by William Sampson who was Orr's leading defence counsel. The author signed himself as *Humanitas* and entered into inordinate detail in the explicit hope that an artist would transform his pen picture into an actual portrait. From this we learn that Orr was tall at 6 feet 2 inches and was, in terms of whether he was lean or fat, 'tending towards the latter', a judgement which concurs with Wheatley's statement. His eyes were brown, his face free from blemishes and his nose 'inclined to the aquiline, though very little slightly'. *Humanitas* was most impressed by his 'bold and martial gait, his erect carriage' and 'his alert and easy motion'. William Orr's clothing was recorded to an almost minute detail, indeed it seems that Orr's personal appearance and deportment during his confinement were very important not only to William Orr but to his supporters. 'His apparel appeared to be all new and fashionable; his shirt and stock were remarkably white, and the ruffle at his breast seemed to have been plaited with great nicety and care; his coat was blue; his waistcoat was a fancy pattern, the ground of which was buff; his breeches were black kersimere; stockings were white silk and worsted, with small stripes of blue; his shoes were tied with black tape. He wore his hair short, and well powdered, with a fashionable round hat, which he sometimes changed for a turkey-leather cap trimmed with rich fur, and tied with a green ribbon.' All in all *Humanitas* wondered that, 'it is a question if a finer fellow could have been found' than William Orr.

The second description is certainly less flattering although it is not completely at odds with the notion that William Orr was concerned with his appearance. It came from the Rev. Macartney's son, Arthur Chichester Macartney, who followed in his father's footsteps to become a Church of Ireland cleric through the patronage of the Donegall family. Some thirty odd years after the 1798 rebellion, Arthur provided R.R. Madden his description of William Orr and his brother Samuel as well as his memories of the Battle of Antrim. Madden in turn reprinted these, but a comparison of the printed version of the description of William Orr with Madden's original notes on his conversation with Arthur Macartney shows that Madden censored many of Arthur's opinions. The note concerning William Orr as given by Macartney is reprinted here in full. 'William Orr was made out as a patriot of great and noble qualities and was looked upon as a martyr. In fact he was a very ordinary man, a wild and dissipated young man of very loose morals and very moderate abilities; a frequenter of cockfights, drinking bouts in public houses and a fair-going boisterous sporting young man, popular among his class – irregular in his habits and of very moderate abilities.'

While it might be easier to warm to this person rather than the almost foppish individual described by *Humanitas*, one has to take Macartney's and indeed both descriptions with a pinch of salt. Macartney was very much of the Ascendancy class in Ireland and looked on William Orr as an upstart who presumed to overturn Macartney's well ordered society in Ireland where patronage was the accepted way of doing things. Other details which Macartney told Madden do not tally exactly with other accounts, including his description of William Orr's arrest. Earlier we have seen how Robert Macartney described the arrest for the benefit of his father and this letter makes no mention at all of any role for his brother Arthur. Yet Arthur claimed to Madden that he had been part of the raiding party and implied that it was done on his own initiative. He also gives the time of Orr's arrrest as in the morning, but Robert Macartney's letter, written the following day, stated it took place at night. Arthur stated that William Orr was found hiding in an oat bin while Robert Macartney wrote he was found in a press or large cupboard.[9]

A year passed before William Orr was brought to trial, as his case was not heard in the Carrickfergus Lent Assizes of 1797 but put back to September 1797. By then, the Crown authorities in Belfast had worked hard to exclude United Irish sympathisers from the jury and there survives the notorious jury list of the time in which suspect jurors are defined under three categories: 'timid men, disaffected and bad in every sense of the word'. The Crown had assembled a strong prosecution team headed by the Attorney General, Arthur Wolfe. Orr was defended by John Philpot Curran, a leading advocate of his day, William Sampson and James McGucken. The evidence against him was that of Wheatley and Lindsay, who could not be shaken from their account. The trial was short, only a day was taken up with evidence and statements, and the jury was sent away in the evening to consider their verdict throughout the night. Despite the Crown's meticulous preparations, the jury at first refused to return any verdict at all. Only after they had been sent out three times by the judge, was the foreman induced to utter the guilty verdict. Judge Barry Yelverton, formerly a patriot or reform MP for Carrickfergus, but now well tuned to the Government's wishes, affected to shed tears as he sentenced William Orr to death. From the dock Orr denied his guilt and claimed that he was the victim of perjured evidence.[10]

Given the nature of the evidence against William Orr, the basis for his claim of innocence deserves some scrutiny. No one, not even Bigger, has denied that the two soldiers were sworn as United Irishmen or that William Orr was present. The cross-examination of Wheatley, as reproduced by Bigger from a pamphlet written by William Sampson, one of the defence team, was hardly severe and the defence case swung on arcane points of law concerning the legality of the Insurrection Act and that the defendant should have been charged with high treason. The soldiers' statements indicate that they were not *agent-provocateurs* sent to Antrim to incriminate Orr, as Bigger has suggested, for their evidence only came to light by chance. The magistrates in Derry, who took their first statement, were unaware of the Orrs' identities and it is the Rev. Macartney who identified them positively. He had been resident in Antrim for over 20 years and, for part of that time, agent to the Massereene estates around the town, so he would have been well aware who the Orrs were. While Macartney had many faults, there is nothing in his career to suggest that he was either vindictive or a deliberate fabricator of evidence and, as subsequent pages will show, he was capable of kindness on behalf of his political opponents. In taking their evidence, Macartney must have had good reasons for believing that the two soldiers were referring to William Orr, even if they could not identify him by name. James Hope's identification of McKeever as the man who did the swearing, as has been discussed, would have been the ideal evidence for the Derry magistrates to obtain from Wheatley and Lindsay, but their statements did not so identify him. Perhaps William Orr's claim that he was a victim of perjured evidence was based on the soldiers' testimony that they were coerced into swearing, which is unlikely given the leisurely nature of their time in Antrim, while James Campbell's jocular statement about throwing aristocrats into his draw well was presented in court as a serious point. On a legalistic level, Orr may have considered that, as the two soldiers had been first sworn in by his cousin John Orr, he, William, could not be guilty of swearing Hugh Wheatley as a United man as he already was one.[11]

William Orr was sentenced to die on 7 October, some 17 days after the verdict was given and, in the intervening period, frenetic attempts were made to save his life. Some jurors swore they had been plied with strong whiskey which had made them ill in the hot and stifling jury room. Another swore he had been pressurised by James MacNaughton from North Antrim into returning a guilty verdict, while another claimed he had only concurred with the verdict after MacNaughton's assurance that Orr would not be executed. Yelverton curtly rejected all these statements as grounds for upsetting the verdict. A Presbyterian minister, Rev. Elder from Rasharkin, claimed that he had offered spiritual support to Wheatley, who was contemplating suicide. This had allegedly happened in April 1796 and therefore before the soldiers arrived in Derry and well before they were exposed. Elder's statement seems only to suggest that he, Elder, was a United Irishman, whom the pair had contacted on their journey to Derry. What is not in doubt is that both fencibles received considerable sums of money from the Government. In a begging letter to Dublin Castle, Wheatley claimed he had been driven from his regiment by threats that he was a traitor, having taken the United Irish oath, and was destitute in Maybole in Ayrshire. For still obscure reasons, the Rev. Macartney repaired to Dublin to intercede on Orr's behalf but, when asked to swear that Orr was innocent, he balked at this and his mission failed. Attempts were allegedly made to bribe to jailer with an offer of 900 guineas if he would connive at Orr's escape.[12]

William Orr's only real hope was to admit his guilt, for which he might expect that his sentence would be commuted and to this end his brother James, the Constable from Randalstown, made strenuous efforts to get William to confess to his charge. It seemed he had succeeded for the *Belfast Newsletter* of the 2nd October carried a report that Orr had signed a confession. However, although a signed confession existed, William Orr repudiated it and his brother James had to admit that he had forged it. The confusion generated by these events brought two postponements of the execution date, first to the 10th and then the 14th October.

While there were many who wanted to save Orr's life, there were those who were determined that he should lose it and these men became increasingly alarmed when it seemed that Orr would avoid death. Yelverton, who had appeared to weep as he sentenced Orr, was writing to Dublin to state he was sure of the Orr's guilt. General Gerald Lake had been given the task of disarming Ulster and had spent the previous year seeking out both arms and rebels in Down and Antrim. Lake's view was clear: if the Government failed to carry out a sentence obtained in an open court, it would render it impossible to obtain future convictions from County Antrim juries. As no one had been executed at the recent Down Assizes, one almost senses that, for Lake, Orr's execution would be the only opportunity of demonstrating that interference with the military would not be tolerated.

The view-point of such ultras was critical and the government in Dublin Castle eventually set its sights against any leniency to Orr. On the eve of the execution, the messenger who arrived in Carrickfergus was not carrying a reprieve but an order for immediate execution. On the following day William Orr was hanged from the 'three sisters', a triangular arrangement of standing stones which stood by the sea shore on Gallows Green beside the road from Carrickfergus to Belfast. He was accompanied to his death by Adam Hill, the Presbyterian minister of Ballynure and William Stavely who was the Covenanting minister of Knockbracken, in the Castlereagh Hills of County Down. Stavely was a native of Ferniskey, not far from Kells in County Antrim but his wife, Mary Donald, provides a line of contact with William Orr at Farranshane, for she was brought up in the Donald family farm at Irishtown, a townland adjacent to Farranshane. To his cost, Stavely had run with the United Irish hare and been imprisoned in the first half of 1797. Undaunted by this experience, he had, on his release, joined a defence support committee for County Down United prisoners, while the *Black Book of the Rebellion* shows that he attended a County Committee meeting in December 1797.[13]

Even after the execution James Orr did not completely abandon hope of saving his brother, for he organised an attempt to resuscitate the corpse in a house not far from Carrickfergus. When told that the attempt was a hopeless one, James 'fell to the ground as if he had been struck by a weapon'. He must have been close to his older brother, for in addition to this attempt, he had done his utmost to remit the sentence of death and he was an executor to William's estate, along with William's brother-in-law (or perhaps father-in-law) John Greer of Duneane and the Rev. Alexander Montgomery of Mill Row. The body was taken to the Ballynure Meeting House of Adam Hill, where it was waked and, on the following day, was buried in the Orr burial plot in Templepatrick Graveyard. The crowds which lined the route had to be dispersed by the soldiers.[14]

For 200 years his grave carried no memorial to his name, indeed the Orrs as a family seem to have been very happy to forgo headstones in Templepatrick. The Madden papers in the library of Trinity College Dublin contain a note to Madden sent by Mary Ann McCracken which contains an 'epitaph intended for the tomb of Wm. Orr'. Miss McCracken wrote that she had been informed that Wolfe Tone had written it. It reads as follows:

'Sacred to the memory of William Orr who was offered up at
Carrickfergus on Sat. the 14th October 1797.

An awful sacrifice to Irish liberty on the altar of British tyranny by the
hands of perjury, through the influence of corruption and the connivance
of partial justice. Irishmen when you forget him, his wrongs, his death,
his cause, not [these] avenge, may you be debarred that liberty he sought
and [be you] forgotten in the liberty of nations!

No, Irishmen let us leave him in steadfast memory. Let his fate nerve
the martial arm to wreak the wrongs of injured Erin and [uphold] her
undoubted claims. Let Orr be the watchword of Liberty.'[15]

William Orr was the first United Irishman to be executed but, if his
death was intended as a demonstration of the might of the State, it soon
became a public relations disaster of epic proportions. The suspect or at
least unsupported nature of the evidence, the packing of and then
intimidation of the jury led to the portrayal of his death as judicial murder.
The dignified manner in which Orr was permitted to meet his death only
added to his reputation as a martyr to tyranny. Perhaps in deference to
local feelings, he had not been subjected to the macabre paraphernalia of
later executions, where the condemned man was first compelled to don
the grave shrouds in which he was to be buried and then taken bound in a
open cart to the place of execution. In contrast, Orr had been not been
pinioned but had been permitted to travel to his execution in a closed
carriage accompanied by Stavely and Hill. To make matters worse, he
had composed a 'Dying Declaration', which was published and circulated.
Soon commemorative material was being produced, encompassing
memorial cards, rings and silk embroidered rosettes. William Drennan
composed his famous poem *The Wake of William Orr*. But most lasting of
all was the rallying cry which his death bequeathed to United Irishmen
throughout Ireland – Remember Orr!

THE DYING DECLARATION

OF

WILLIAM ORR, of Ferranſhane, in the County of Antrim, Farmer.

TO THE PUBLICK.

MY FRIENDS AND COUNTRYMEN,

IN the Thirty-first Year of my Life, I have been sentenced to die upon the Gallows, and this Sentence has been in Pursuance of a Verdict of Twelve Men, who should have been indifferently and impartially chosen; how far they have been so, I leave to that County from which they have been chosen, to determine; and how far they have discharged their Duty, I leave to their God and to themselves.————They have in pronouncing their Verdict, thought proper to recommend me as an Object of humane Mercy; in Return, I pray to God, if they have erred, to have Mercy upon them. The Judge, who condemned me, humanely shed Tears in uttering my Sentence, but whether he did wisely in so highly commending the wretched Informer, who swore away my Life, I leave to his own cool reflection, solemnly assuring him and all the World, with my dying Breath, That that Informer was foresworn. The Law under which I suffer, is surely a severe one; may the Makers and Promoters of it be justified in the Integrity of their Motives and the Purity of their own Lives—by that Law, I am stamped a Felon, but my heart disdains the Imputation. My comfortable Lot and industrious Course of Life, best refute the Charge of being an Adventurer for Plunder: but if to have loved my Country, to have known its Wrongs, to have felt the Injuries of the persecuted Catholic, and to have united with them and all other Religious Persuasions in the most orderly and least sanguinary Means of procuring Redress:—If those be Felonies, I am a Felon, but not otherwise. Had my Councils, (for whose honorable Exertions I am indebted) prevailed in their Motion to have me tried for High Treason, rather than under the *Insurrection Law*, I should have been intitled then to a full Defence and my Actions and Intentions have been better vindicated, but that was refused, and I must now submit to what has passed.

TO the generous Protection of my Country, I leave a beloved Wife, who has been constant and true to me, and whose Grief for my Fate has already nearly occasioned her Death. I leave five living Children, who have been my Delight—may they love their Country as I have done, and die for it, if needful.

LASTLY, a false and ungenerous Publication having appeared in a Newspaper, stating, certain alledged Confessions of Guilt on my Part, and thus striking at my Reputation, which is dearer to me than Life, I take this solemn Method of contradicting that Calumny.————I was applied to by the High Sheriff and the Rev. William Bristow, Sovereign of Belfast, to make a Confession of Guilt, who used entreaties to that Effect; this I peremptorily refused; did I think myself guilty, I should be free to confess it, but on the contrary, I glory in my Innocence.

I trust that all my virtuous countrymen will bear me in their kind Remembrance, and continue true and faithful to each other, as I have been to all of them, with this last Wish of my Heart, nothing doubting of the Success of that Cause for which I suffer, and hoping for God's merciful Forgiveness of such Offences as my frail Nature may have at any Time betrayed me into. I die in Peace and Charity with all Mankind.

WILLIAM ORR.

CARRICKFERGUS GAOL,
OCTOBER 5, 1797.

N. B. *The above Declaration was made and read by* WILLIAM ORR, *in the Presence of the Rev. Mr. Savage.*

CHAPTER 3 FOOTNOTES

1 Joseph Orr of Derry fled to France late in 1797 when he was a member of the UI National Executive. References to his time in France can be found in Elliot (1982). There is no evidence of any family link between him and the Orrs of Antrim.

2 For Hope's reference to McKeever see Madden (1858) *The United Irishmen – Their lives and times,* iv, 254. William McKeever was evidently set free after his arrest in Derry, for he appears in the spring of 1798 as the Derry delegate to the Ulster Provincial Committee. Incredibly he was still using the alias of Campbell and, after a less than glorious rising in Maghera, he fled to America. (Mac Suibhne, 1998 & Stewart, 1995). He was also listed under Fugitive Bill in late 1798 as 'Wm. Campbell alias McKeevers of Upperlands (HO/100/66/350 & Madden *op. cit.* i, 581). Bigger in *Remember Orr* (p27) mentions Hope's reference but mis-spells McKeever as McIvor.

3 Two judges sat at William Orr's trial, Tankerville Chamberlain & Barry Yelverton (Stewart, 1995). For Macartney's time as rector of All Saints Parish Church, Antrim see Glendinning (1996).

4 There were two Orr families belonging to Mill Row resident in Creavery. Magill's *Names of seat-holders* gives lists Templepatrick as the burying ground of John Orr of Creavery while the other Orr family in Creavery were buried in Connor. Magill gives no indication of any genealogical link between these two families.

5 The transcript of this document given in Dickson (1970) *Revolt in the North* (p1777-182) was shortened considerably by omitting sections and by replacing parts of the text. Hyndman's active involvement is not mentioned and a minor point is that Dickson's version states that John Orr 'stood them a drink', a phrase which is not in the original. Macartney had the benefit of some legal training, having obtained a doctor of laws degree in 1789, and the transcript of his statement presented here has been shortened by omitting his liberal use of the words *said* and *aforesaid*. Occasionally these have been substituted with *the* and *this* marked in italics.

6 Wheatley's placing his being sworn in William Orr's own house agrees with James Hope's account in Madden (*op. cit.*). In contrast, Bigger's *Remember Orr* states the meeting was held in Jack Gourlay's barn adjacent to William Orr's farm. Bigger's researches were hampered by the fact that none of the surviving Orrs took him into their confidence. Undaunted he pursued his investigations around Farranshane, where he became friendly with a William Crawford and his account relies on what Crawford told him. He claimed Crawford's source was Jack Gourlay who had related the story to Crawford in his boyhood. As Crawford, who was born around 1840, was likely the source of some of the erroneous statements in *Remember Orr*, his version of the fateful meeting may also have become rather garbled over intervening period of some 100 years. According to Crawford, the meeting was attended by Gourlay, William Orr, Dick Roy, Andy Parker, David McQuillan and David Campbell and others.

7 John Staples was an MP for County Antrim. Smith (1888) in *Historical gleanings in Antrim and neighbourhood* (pp 17-18) gives an oral history account from a lady who, as a girl, lived at Farranshane in 1796 which suggests that the soldiers first went there the night Orr was arrested. Her story is not implausible, as *after* arresting William Orr, the soldiers went to search out James Campbell who did live beside Farranshane.

8 See *Northern Star* reports in Clifford (1992). *Prison adverts and potatoe diggings*.

9 Humanitas pen portrait from Bigger's *Remember Orr* pp 9-10. Arthur Macartney's

opinion of William Orr in TCD MS 873/267. The Madden précis of Macartney's opinion was: 'William Orr was looked upon as a person of singularly great and noble qualities. The fact is he was a man of very moderate abilities; athletic in his frame, active and somewhat of a sporting character among his class.' (*Antrim & Down in '98*, p54). Arthur Macartney's account of William Orr's arrest was: 'Dr [Rev. George] Macartney being obliged to go to England, his son, now the vicar of Belfast [Arthur Macartney], hearing that Orr's father was dying, and that William Orr would likely be at home, mentioned the circumstances to an officer, who accompanied him to the father's house at 10 o'clock *in the morning* and surrounded the house with soldiers. William Orr was not to be found; at length, on searching an outhouse, he was discovered in an oatbin'. (*Antrim & Down in '98*, p 54).

10 Bigger's *Remember Orr* details the trial as reported in *The Press*.

11 Bigger's theory was that Lord Castlereagh who was acting on information provided by Samuel Turner had set the soldiers on the trail of William Orr. Immediately after the swearing in, the soldiers then went voluntarily to the Rev. Macartney to give their statement. Apart from contradicting the true time-scale of soldiers' statements, this is an impossible scenario as Turner only became a Government informer and double agent late in 1797, after William Orr was executed. Malcomson (1972) states that the 2nd Earl of Massereene had entrusted the affairs of his Antrim estates to Macartney in the 1780s (p103).

12 Interventions by Elder and Macartney in Madden *Antrim and Down in '98* p54 and Lecky, *A history of Ireland* vol. IV p109, who also refers to Lake's letter to Pelham concerning an attempt to bribe the jailer.

13 For details of Stavely's activities in County Down see Robinson (1998) *North Down and Ards in 1798* and the Black Book of the Rebellion (PRONI D/272/1). Stavely's own and rather more sanitised account is reprinted in Dunlop (1993) pages 19-23.

14 The account of James Orr's attempt to revive the corpse is in Smith (1996) *Memories of '98* p17. One of Francis Bigger's more evocative lines in *Remember Orr* (p.51) was that William Orr was buried in Templepatrick beside 'his favourite sister, Ally Orr', a line which has been repeated rather uncritically by local historians. The headstone to Ally Orr in Templepatrick is the only one to a member of the Orr family and gives her age as 51 when she died in 1791. This makes her 26 years older than her supposed brother William Orr, not an impossible difference but nevertheless an improbable one. Magill's Orr family tree lists no sister of William Orr called Ally, but gives his mother's name as Alicia. It is most likely therefore that the headstone refers to William Orr's mother. This demonstrates again the carelessness of Bigger's approach to matters of detail, for the association of the headstone with William Orr's mother was known in Bigger's time. In the late 1890s Alice Milligan & Ana Johnston (alias Ethna Carberry) combined to produce the *Shan Van Vocht*, a Nationalist magazine, to which Bigger contributed. The *Shan Van Vocht* for 3 July 1896 describes 'an excursion to the scene of the Antrim Fight and Patriot Graves' during which wreaths were laid on the graves visited. In referring to William Orr's grave the reporter wrote: 'It bears the simple inscription – Here lyeth the body of Ally Orr. It his mothers grave'. I am indebted to Bríghid Mac Seáin for bringing this article to my attention.

15 Epitaph to William Orr in TCD MS 873/33. I have inserted the word 'uphold' to replace what seems to be 'upert' in the manuscript and 'these' to replace 'there'.

4
John Orr – pike maker

In 1796 General Lake was sent to Ulster with the specific task of disarming it. A particular target was the retrieval of a set of six cannon which the United men were known to have commandeered from the Belfast company of the old Irish Volunteers. The search for these cannon was relentless, with many fruitless swoops. General Lake described how his troops were like mountain goats as they combed the Cave Hill above Belfast. Mill ponds were drained in the hope of finding the elusive cannons. Eventually perseverance was rewarded by the retrieval of four – a letter to Dublin described how they had been coated with tallow to preserve them against rust – but two remained hidden under the pulpit of the Presbyterian Church in Templepatrick, only a few hundred yards from the grave of William Orr.[1] Faced with a dearth of firearms, the strategists of the United Irishmen proposed the use of pikes, which they supposed would have a fair chance of repelling soldiers, particularly cavalry. The pike's advantage was that it could be made in the blacksmith forges which dotted the Ulster countryside. In addition, the pike-head was small and could be easily hidden. Accordingly Lake's troops subjected blacksmiths to many searches including John Orr the blacksmith of Creavery.

When Bigger was collecting his material for *Remember Orr*, W.S. Smith, the minister of the Old Presbyterian Congregation in Antrim, was penning a series of articles entitled *Memories of '98* which Bigger included in the *Ulster Journal of Archaeology*. They were based on reminiscences of the Rebellion around Antrim which Smith had collected and one of them concerns John Orr of Creavery, who had evaded capture after William Orr's arrest but had evidently fallen off the wanted list. He owned a blacksmith's shop in Creavery but did not operate it personally. One day, when he called at the forge, he found his tenant making pike heads with the help of an apprentice. Given what is known of John Orr and his involvement with the swearing in of Wheatley and Lindsay and his behaviour after the Rebellion, this manufacturing endeavour need not have been a surprise to him – perhaps he was making sure that his tenant was making pikes. As he was leaving the forge, Orr saw a company of soldiers approaching and he dashed back to get the smith to remove the pikes. For their part, the smith and his assistant were taking no chances and they fled to the adjoining hills, leaving John Orr with the incriminating evidence.

This building in Creavery was originally a blacksmith's forge and so may have been the one owned by John Orr in 1799.

Thinking quickly and knowing that he could be hung at the door of his forge if he was caught making pikes, Orr donned the blacksmith's apron and threw the pikes back into the fire. Furiously he worked at the bellows to raise the coals to a white-hot heat and cause the pike heads to melt. By the time the soldiers entered the forge, the heat had rendered the pikes a mass of molten metal. John Orr, complete with the authentic sweat of a smith interrupted at his work, was able to assure his visitors that he was but an innocent blacksmith in the process of making nothing more harmful than a spade. After some questioning and a brief search the soldiers left.[2]

Richard Fleming of Fountain Street in Antrim claimed he heard John Orr retell this story 'again and again'. Whatever the truth behind the story, John Orr was not to escape so lightly in another encounter with soldiers. He had become head of the family in Creavery when his father died in 1797, the same year as his younger brother, William the watch-maker, returned from Dublin. Around 1803, William compiled some notes concerning the Rebellion and for the 1 June 1798 he recorded:

> Major Seddon comes to brother's house with troop of dragoons, threatens to burn the place if did not surrender a number of pikes and other arms that he was informed that I knew of. The house is cleared for him and the family disperse. He sends for me to speak to him.[3]

The burning of John Orr's house in Creavery left the family homeless only six days before County Antrim was to rise in rebellion. Newgrove is a farm some 10 miles from Creavery in Ballygarvey, between Ballymena and Broughshane and was to be William Orr's home when he died. The Wilson family who lived there from the 1860s, have a tradition that William Orr stayed at Newgrove just before the Rebellion. At that time, it was home to the prosperous Duffin family who owed their wealth to linen. William Duffin had been prominent in politics as Deputy Governor of County Antrim in 1794 but his son, William, was more radical and was the leader of the United Irishmen in Broughshane. There appears to be no family relationship between the Duffins and the Orrs, so if the Orr family found refuge at Newgrove, it is likely to have been through a political or linen connection.[4]

The Creavery incident occurred six days before the rising began in Antrim but eight days after the Rebellion had erupted in the south of Ireland. Attacks on the mail coaches leaving Dublin on 23 May were to be a signal for a general rising throughout Ireland, but the days following had been disastrous to the rebel cause. The key to the rising had been the capture of Dublin Castle and destruction of the nerve centre of government in Ireland. This objective had failed utterly and insurrections in the counties surrounding Dublin had been similarly crushed or contained. Only in Wexford and south Wicklow were the rebels enjoying tangible successes. To the men fighting there, the absence of news of a rising in the North, the cradle of the United Irish movement was inexplicable, but the failure of Antrim to rise was no accident for the leadership there, under Robert Simms as Adjutant General, was determined not to hazard an insurrection without the support of a French landing.[5]

The policy of Simms was not sustainable for, as the days passed, the pressure from the rank and file to rise mounted inexorably. On 1 June matters came to a head at a meeting of the County Antrim leadership held in Parkgate, about five miles from Antrim. Initially the meeting was disturbed by a troop of soldiers passing through the village but it reconvened about a mile away in Dr Agnew's inn in Templepatrick. Faced with demands to rise, Simms resigned and, as none of the others present would offer themselves as a replacement, it was decided to meet again two days later. One aspect of William Orr's account, given above, is that it shows he was not at home in Creavery when Major Seddon arrived on 1 June. In addition, Seddon, who was the commander of the unit of 22nd Dragoons based in Antrim, suspected William as being more directly involved in the hiding of arms than his brother John. William's absence from home on 1 June and his friendship with Duffin, raises the possibility that he was one those who met in Parkgate and Templepatrick that day.

Two days later the Antrim leadership met again, this time near Ballyclare, but still could not elect a leader. The meeting was split and, by one account, a majority approved of not rising until the French would appear on the scene. It seems that the minority, buoyed up by support from those waiting for the decision, reconvened and installed Henry Joy McCracken as their leader. The decision to rise was not taken until 5 June but from then on events unfolded with a reckless haste.

CHAPTER 4 FOOTNOTES

1 Letter from Lisburn 3 June 1798 *Reb. Papers* 620/38/36

2 Smith, W.S. (1996) *Memories of '98.* pages 2-3. Smith's articles appeared in a number of issues of the *Ulster Journal of Archaeology* of 1895 and were combined in a single volume by the Mid-Antrim Historical Group in 1996.

3 From *Diary of an Irish Rebel.* (SRNSW ref: SZ851; Reel 2504)

4 Kenny, *William Orr, Newgrove and elsewhere*, unpublished ms & Kenny (1988) *As the crow flies over rough terrain.* p145.

5 Details of the meetings which led up to the rising in Antrim are taken from Stewart (1995) pp 60-68.

5
'to effect a Revolution'

For many of those who took part, the 1798 rising in Antrim was referred to as *The Turnout* but in some places it is also remembered as *The Hurry*, indicating the sudden decision to rise. The appointed day, Thursday 7 June 1798, dawned clear and sunny and, from an early hour, it was evident that the countryside of County Antrim was going to rise. Men could be observed moving along lanes and roads armed with a motley assortment of weapons: pikes, guns and pitch-forks. Despite the delayed decision to rise, the United Irishmen had a tolerably well thought-out plan of action to follow. Throughout the county there were hill-top assembly points to which rebels were to rendezvous, the most notable of which was at Donegore. This was a sensible starting point for the prospective citizen army which had until then trained and assembled in small groups and in secret. From these assembly points, groups were to seize those towns and villages which were slightly or not at all defended. The climax of the day, which seems to have been planned to proceed at a rather leisurely pace, was to attack Antrim town at 2 o'clock in the afternoon. By overcoming the garrison, the largest outside Carrickfergus, Belfast and Lisburn, the United Irish command would gain control of the main roads north and west from Belfast. A meeting of the County Antrim magistrates was also planned for Antrim on 7 June. Seizing the magistrates there, would not only remove the representatives of civil authority in the County but provide the rebels with high-profile hostages with whom they could bargain with the Government.[1]

In Duneane parish, one of the meeting points is still recognizable where a farm lane joins the not much larger Ballynafey Road at a point where, in times past, other farm lanes, now obliterated, also met. Opposite the lane-way, a cattle house occupies the site of a farmstead formerly belonging to the Warden family. Until the 1950s, when it succumbed to a storm, the large oak which stood opposite the farmstead was known as Warden's Oak. In 1998 the remains of its massive trunk could be found surrounded by nettles at the edge of the road. It was under this tree that the Insurgents assembled on that June morning and those who met there may have been part of the company of men which stopped at 11 a.m. outside a spirit-grocer's shop in the adjacent townland of Lismacluskey. They were led by William Cook, who stopped his company for refreshments outside his shop. Whiskey was procured and the ranks gave up the fervent toast 'Here's to your health Captain Cook' before marching on to a rebel assembly point on Groggan mountain, a high point on the road from Randalstown to Portglenone. At around 600 feet high, Groggan is hardly a mountain and the hill-top is farmland intermingled with peat bog. It was here that the insurgents had a training ground, well hidden from passing view, which today is a field known to local farmers as the Parade Ground.[2]

On 7 June 1798, Robert Magill was a nine-year old boy attending school in the village of Broughshane but the master dismissed the class early at noon and Magill went home. Sitting down for his dinner, the sound of drums came from the street and Robert ran out to see what was happening but, when he asked the drummer the reason for his display, he received the curt reply – 'You'll know soon enough'. Soon rebels with their guns and pikes and guns glittering in the bright sunshine entered the village unopposed to assemble at Tullymore on the edge of the village. William Duffin of Newgrove was at their head and the troop included Magill's schoolmaster, Mr Alexander. Later that week, Magill recalled how he saw 'Captain Duffin' giving an order for his men to wear green cockades.[3]

Samuel Orr of Kilbegs was to lead his men on an attack on Randalstown. Orr later claimed to have only received the order to rise on the previous day and getting his men together at such short notice was not without problems. One of his subordinates, Robert McGowan, was later to state

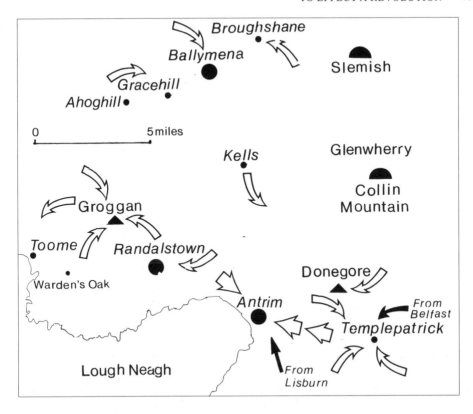

The Rising of 7 June 1798 in Mid Antrim. The open arrows show the main movements of United Irishmen. The solid arrows indicate the approach of troops from Belfast and Lisburn.

that he only turned out after Samuel Orr threatened to 'cut off his ears if he would not go and bring others to join with them'. The defending force in Randalstown consisted of a few yeomen headed by Thomas Hamilton Jones of Moneyglass and Lieutenant Ellis. The yeomen soon took refuge in the Market or Linen House, which was then on the main street, a fairly narrow thoroughfare. From there they exchanged a largely ineffectual gun-fire with their attackers and it was not until the yeomen's ammunition was exhausted that the rebels gained the upper hand. Even then, the yeomen could only be induced to surrender after the rebels placed straw in the open ground floor of the Market House and set fire to it. Then, and with no little difficulty from the flames and those attackers who wanted to murder the yeomen there and then, the loyalist defenders were rescued, captured and dispatched as prisoner-hostages to the camp at Groggan.[4]

Victory was not achieved in Randalstown until noon and the next stage of the plan was for Samuel Orr to have his men at Antrim for 2 p.m. Here they would attack the town from the west in support of the Sixmilewater forces, led by Henry Joy McCracken, which were to attack from the east and north of the town. To the south in Crumlin, which lay on the southern route from Lisburn to Antrim, the insurgents were meant to hold the line against reinforcements from Blaris, the main army camp in the North.[5]

John Orr of The Folly was the most senior of the Orrs who would take the field on 7 June when he must have been around 60 years of age but that morning saw him in an irritable mood. Like his nephew Samuel, John had to assemble his men and, although he lived less than a mile from Antrim, he was under orders to march them four miles away from the town to Templepatrick, where they would rendezvous with McCracken's forces. His poor temper was due to a number of factors. Firstly, as he had explained to a fellow rebel, Henry O'Hara, he had had little sleep, having been up all night making shafts for pike heads – testimony to the lack of preparedness of the rebel army around Antrim. A more pressing problem was that many of Orr's fellow citizens either did not seem to be aware of the momentous events planned for that day or, if they were, nevertheless

The Folly. John Orr's farm house at The Folly is long gone in Antrim but the name lives on as a residential street, off the Greystone Road.

they were determined to go about their business regardless. Such was the case of John English, who was on his way into Antrim on the morning of 7 June. When passing the avenue leading down to The Folly, he encountered John Orr who stopped English's horse. Orr told him that it would be impossible to get into Antrim as the hedges and ditches along the road were lined with armed men who would kill him if he tried to pass. English was having none of this and replied that, if he must be killed, it should be near home for he was determined to go to Antrim. Orr stormed off to his house threatening to get his gun and shoot English himself, who in turn continued into the town.[6]

Gathering up his men was not without its frustrations. Threats could not induce Mary Hunter at Drumacalliagh to send her sons to join the Insurgents even though Orr promised to set her house ablaze if she did not. He had more luck with this approach when dealing with Henry Anderson who had decided that his time would be better spent hoeing his potatoes. When Orr arrived at his house, armed with a gun, he could see Anderson in the field and he signalled for him to come. Anderson feigned not to see the 'come on' waves of Orr and only left the field when he was called. Why, asked Orr, had Anderson not turned out when he knew that 'the country was up'? Anderson at first refused to join but changed his mind when Orr threatened to burn his house.[7]

The circuit taken on this recruiting march was not the most direct route to Templepatrick, for Mary Hunter lived near Loughanmore, which is close to Donegore. On the way Orr, met a rebel 'orderly' who told him to hurry up and get to Templepatrick in order to meet up with men from Roughfort and Killead, otherwise they would miss the 2 p.m. deadline for the attack on Antrim. In Templepatrick, they and forces from Killead to the south, met up with McCracken's men from Roughfort. One of the volunteer cannon was retrieved from beneath the pulpit of the Old Presbyterian Church in the village and mounted on a makeshift gun carriage. The rebel forces also re-organised and those men who had fire-arms, including John Orr, formed a unit of musket men. Offers to take command were apparently there for the taking and both John Orr and James Hope claimed to have refused such offers, each being content to line up in the ranks. With these hardly auspicious preparations McCracken's Army of Ulster set off for Antrim, led by 18 men from Roughfort.[8]

Approaching from the east, Antrim town consisted largely of one long street, which went downhill through the Scotch Quarter, past the Old

Presbyterian Church on the right and then, on the left hand side, past the Church of Ireland. It then levelled out and widened into the High Street proper. This section is perfectly straight from the Church of Ireland to Market Square, which was bounded on one side by the walls of Antrim Castle gardens. In Market Square stood the Court House, where the magistrates were to meet. As they marched into the Scotch Quarter, McCracken's men halted, possibly because they were early and McCracken wanted to wait until another attacking column in Patie's Lane (now Railway Street) headed by John Storey would be place. Jane Lees was willing to state that she saw John Orr standing with the 'common men' for some 15 minutes outside the Old Presbyterian Church, from where they were largely out of sight from the High Street.

The defending force in Antrim was comparatively slight, consisting of forty yeomanry and some dragoons, headed by Major Seddon. In Belfast, General Nugent only received warning of the attack on Antrim at 6 o'clock on the morning of the 7th June. Despite this short notice, within a few hours he had been able to dispatch two columns of reinforcements. Colonel Drummond headed the force which set out from Belfast, while Col. Clavering headed Light Dragoons from the Blaris Camp at Lisburn. An advance party of Clavering's column, headed by Lieutenant Colonel Lumley, pressed ahead and entered Antrim about the same time as McCracken. Lumley's orders were to hold the town until the main army reinforcements arrived, but he had no intention of carrying out a defensive holding operation in Antrim. Rather he would turn defence into attack by means of a cavalry charge on the rebels. This Lumley proceeded to do with disastrous consequences. First he ordered his cannon to be fired at the rebels. The shot was aimed too low as it failed to take account of the rising ground leading to the Scotch Quarter and caused little injury. In any case, at the first sight of the cannon, those at the front of the rebel column had clambered over the graveyard wall which surrounded All Saints Church of Ireland. Others entered the houses opposite and positioned themselves at windows.[9]

Lumley charged, first into a fire of shot from the rebels' sole Volunteer cannon. This did some damage, but either the recoil of the cannon firing or the galloping horses knocked it from its makeshift gun carriage and it played no further part in the day. As the horsemen charged on, they found themselves funnelling into the narrowest section of the street where it passed the church. Here, they were mercilessly attacked by musket fire from the windows of the houses and from the grave-yard. The pikemen

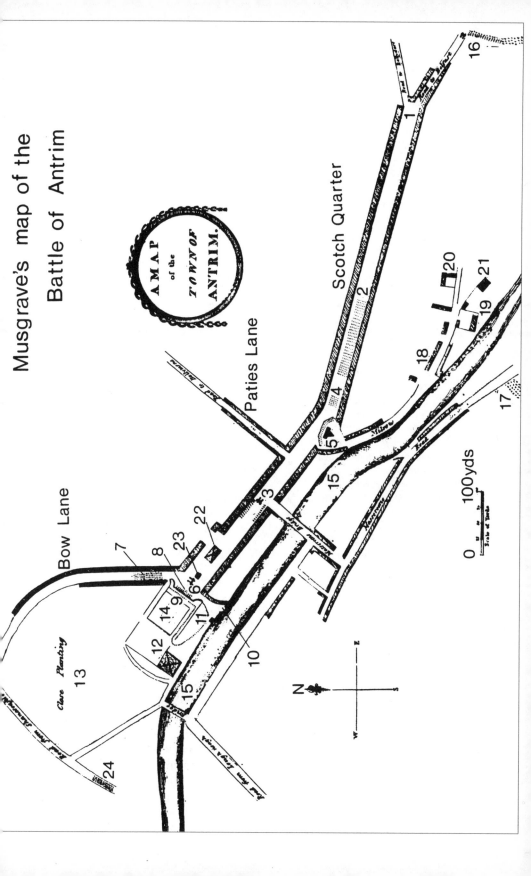

Musgrave's map of the Battle of Antrim

MUSGRAVE'S MAP OF THE BATTLE OF ANTRIM

In 1800 Sir Richard Musgrave produced a map detailing the main events associated with the Battle of Antrim, which is reproduced here. It predates the first Ordnance Survey map of Antrim by over 30 years and, in some minor respects, the alignment of streets as shown is not accurate. The legend given to the map is as follows:

1   Where the rebel columns from Ballyclare and Templepatrick joined.

2   The rebels in close column with a six-pounder in front, when the curricle guns under Lieutenant Neville opened their fire on them

3   Lieutenant Neville, with two six pounders, flanked by the yeomanry and dragoons under Colonel Lumley firing on the rebels.

4   Colonel Lumley charging the rebels after passing the church yard.

5   The church-yard lined with rebels, who are represented by the dotted lines, firing on the dragoons charging as they passed, and among whom they did great execution.

6   The guns under Lieutenant Neville, after retreating from No. 3, firing on the second column of the rebels advancing up Bow-lane.

7   The second rebel column.

8   The dragoons, after charging, drawn up under the dead wall of Lord Massareene's garden, and covered on their flank by a demi bastion.

9   The yeomanry firing over the wall on the rebels who attempted to get possession of the guns at No. 6, after the artillery had abandoned them, and the dragoons had retreated across the river.

10   The watering place over which the dragoons retreated.

11   The entrance to Lord Massareene's court: The dotted lines from it represent the road the yeomanry retreated to take post in the garden where they could only be attacked by the narrow walk through which they got in.

12   Lord Massareene's castle.

13   Lord Massareene's domain.

14   Lord Massareene's walled garden.

15   The Six-mile water.

16   Colonel Durham with the Monaghan militia, and Captain Coulson of the artillery, firing on the rebels retreating by the Ballymena road.

17   The light battalion from Blaris camp under Colonel Clavering drawn up.

18   Distillery.

19   Barracks.

20   Dr Macartney's [Rev. Dr George Macartney home at Belmont].

21   Flour-mills.

22   Market house with the prisoners [the magistrates who had been captured by the rebels].

23   Little guard-house, behind which Lord O'Neill.

24   The rebel column under Colonel [Samuel] Orr.

came into their own, for horses were unable to turn or manoeuvre in the confined space. Facing a massacre, Lumley extricated his horsemen and himself from the battle and abandoned the High Street, retreating back across the Sixmilewater, with losses of over 30 men dead or injured.[10]

Reconstructing the course of subsequent events is not without difficulty as only two combatants have given anything like comprehensive accounts of the battle. One of these was the United Irishman James Hope, who fought from the graveyard in Antrim. The other was Arthur Chichester Macartney, then teenage son of the Rev. George Macartney, who was on duty in Antrim as a yeoman. Some 40 years after the battle both these men provided R.R. Madden with their versions of events. Macartney's version so stung Hope that he penned a quite extensive reply, which added further material about the battle, but unfortunately this does not concur exactly Hope's first version. So, when printed together, there are three versions of the battle. To these can be added a version published by Sir Richard Musgrave in 1800.[11]

When Lumley left the High Street, victory must have seemed to be within McCracken's grasp. The yeomanry force also retreated to the Castle walls in Market Square, abandoning their two cannon. Some of McCracken's men advanced rapidly after them and, on Massereene bridge, which leads south from High Street to Lisburn, they engaged men of the Magheragall Yeoman Cavalry who were driven off. Further down the street they reached the Court House and some magistrates were captured. The chief magistrate, Lord O'Neill, resisted when he was attacked and received, what was to be, a mortal wound from a pike.[12]

It was now a case of so far but no further, for McCracken would begin to realise a flaw in his plan of action. The yeomanry had retreated behind the wall of the Antrim Castle gardens, which bounded the west side of Market Square. Today it presents itself as an ornamental feature, but it is a relict of the 17th century defensive fortifications. The present facing on the wall is a product of the mid-nineteenth century, but restoration work in 1998 revealed, hidden behind this ornamental facade, gun-loops from which the yeomen could fire with near impunity on their attackers. At either end of the wall, cross fire could be directed from the old cannon bastions at anyone foolish enough to try and creep along the foot of the wall. As the advance of his men along High Street halted under the fire of the yeomanry from the Castle Walls, McCracken must have wondered what had happened to Samuel Orr's reinforcements from Randalstown. Orr was supposed to lead his men along Bow Lane which, as its name implies, swept in an arc from the Market Square towards Randalstown. Bow Lane in 1798 was built up on either side for a distance of 600 yards and, from his position in High Street, McCracken had no means of knowing what was going on there.

Different versions have been given of Samuel Orr's actions at Antrim but all agree that he and his men played little or no role in the actual fighting. According to one account, the retreat of Lumley's horsemen

Antrim. This aerial view of Antrim's High Street was taken on a market day early in the 1930s. The layout of the town was little changed from 1798. In the foreground is Antrim Castle (a roofless ruin after the fire of 1921) with the gardens and wall overlooking Market Square and the Court House, where the magistrates were to meet. The spire of All Saints Church is visible at the opposite end of High Street. The Insurgents occupied the graveyard of the church. Bow Lane, renamed Bow Street by 1930, leads onto Market Square. It was along this thoroughfare that the Insurgent attack failed to materialise.

An aerial view of the Castle Gardens, to which the Yeomen retreated after
Col Lumley's cavalry had abandoned the town.

caused Samuel Orr and his men to turn and flee. Musgrave's plan of the Battle of Antrim suggests that Orr's force of some 1500 never entered the town at all and Musgrave states that Orr's men retreated back to Randalstown, frightened, when he heard the sound of cannon from the town. Hope wrote 'Samuel Orr behaved like a coward at Antrim; his flight caused a party headed by McCracken who were proceeding to dislodge a body of yeomen in Lord Massereene's demesne to take flight'. Hope then partially contradicts this by writing that it was the retreat of some of the Ballyclare contingent under yeomanry fire which caused Orr's men to panic and run. Musgrave also describes the retreat of the Ballyclare men down Bow Lane when they were fired on. In 1893, R.M. Young published another very brief account based on an oral history account from relatives of a yeoman. In this version, Orr's men only got as far as the Roman Catholic Chapel, on the very outskirts of the town, at the junction of the roads to Dunsilly and Randalstown shown on Musgrave's map, before retreating on sight of the yeomanry. The yeomanry also turned and ran back to the safety of the Castle Walls.

In considering Samuel Orr's actions, it should be remembered that his men had nearly or completely exhausted their gunpowder in the assault of Randalstown. If they marched along the narrow confines of Bow Lane, effectively armed with only pikes and pitchforks, the wisdom of pressing their attack against the muskets of their opponents from behind the bastion in Market Square would have been unappealing. When Market Square came into view, they would have realised that there they were completely at the mercy of the defenders on the castle walls. Samuel Orr's men retreated to Donegore Hill.[13]

Without knowledge of Orr's actions, it must have dawned on McCracken that he could only hope to dislodge the yeomanry by attacking them from their rear. This decision may account for the lull in the fighting on High Street during which Arthur Macartney and his brother John led a party of yeomen, who sortied out and retrieved the cannon which had been abandoned on the street. To out-flank the yeomanry from Bow Lane, McCracken had to move a force along the back of the houses of High Street, not an easy task given their extensive gardens and vegetable plots. John McGivern, possibly related through marriage to William Orr, had volunteered to lead a party of musket-men to attack the Castle gardens from their rear, where they could not have been easily defended. Indeed, instead of entering Antrim down Bow Lane, had Samuel Orr's men made their advance through the close planting of the Castle Grounds, they may have met with some success.[14]

By now the second great failing of McCracken's strategy was coming into play, for Colonel Durham had arrived on the outskirts of Antrim from Belfast with his infantry, cavalry and artillery. McCracken seems to have given no thought to this possibility and Durham had enjoyed an interrupted march through the deserted countryside, crossing the Sixmilewater River at Dunadry without the slightest resistance. At the same time the main party of the 22nd Dragoons arrived under Col Clavering from the south. These two commanders were able to send messengers to each other and Durham, the senior officer, declined any immediate attempt to retake the town. This was consistent with the British army strategy which was not to take unnecessary risks with its limited and precious man-power – Lumley's impetuous attack was never commended and was described by General Nugent, who had overall command of the North, as 'unfortunate'. Instead Durham from his position, close to what is now the Top of the Town pub in Antrim and overlooking the roofs of the town, ordered his artillery to begin shelling.[15]

Although the first shot fired by Lumley at the start of battle caused little or no injury, it did deplete the rebel ranks. Hope records that McCracken at this time had to leave his command post in the Churchyard to rally troops who were positioned behind him in reserve, i.e. in Antrim's Scotch Quarter. When Lumley's cannon rang out, James Finlay fled down one of the entries which led off the street and headed straight for home. Finlay lived next door to John Orr and the two had marched together into Antrim. James was probably not the only man to have considered that fighting was not all it had been cracked up to be, but those that were left were about to experience a much more terrifying experience, for Durham's bombardment lasted for 30 minutes. At the end of this time, Durham wrote in his official report that 'the rebels were seen flying in different directions'.[16]

Durham's report, written on the eve of the battle, shows that he believed the shelling of the town, followed by sending a detachment of his force to cut off the line of the rebel retreat, were instrumental in causing the rebels to flee Antrim. It does not mention any heroic return to the action which some accounts credit to Lumley. Surprisingly, neither Hope nor Macartney made any reference to the bombardment of Antrim in their accounts. As McCracken and McGivern wended their way through the gardens backing on to the High Street houses, their men started to lose heart and began to flee. Whether they were dispirited by Sam Orr's retreat is very open to debate as from the gardens they still could not see what was going on in

Bow Lane. The sounds of cannon and/or the sight of Durham's men closing in would surely, as Durham implied, have been sufficient for panic to spread through the rebel ranks. In vain McCracken tried to halt the growing rout but the battle was lost.

James Hope seems to have spent the whole of the Battle of Antrim in the Churchyard. As Clavering's men entered the High Street from the south, Hope beat a retreat, but his men kept in good order and reached the Greystone Road on the way to Donegore. Here they had sufficient nerve to stop and face Clavering who, refusing to risk anything, did not force battle. Many of the others who had fled from the town in ones and twos were not so fortunate and were cut down by marauding cavalry. In Antrim town, the Monaghan Militia ran amok, looting and killing perhaps a dozen innocent civilians. Robert Magill's *Names of Seat Holders of the Mill Row Congregation* records only two names as having died in Antrim on the 7 June: a man named Johnson and his daughter, who were cut down by the soldiers. Hope claimed that the actual fighting in Antrim cost the United men only six or so casualties, far less than experienced by the defending force, and that it was only when the insurgents fled in disorder did heavy casualties occur. Estimates of the numbers who fell on the 7th June in Antrim range up to 500 but most accounts settle at between 150 and 200 dead.[17]

Today those with an interest in local history can debate the course of the Battle of Antrim, but the outcome of the day can not be doubted. Those who were loyal to George III, King of Ireland, England and Scotland were victorious. Those who wanted a new and democratic order in Ireland to which Protestant, Catholic and Dissenter could claim an equal allegiance were defeated. William Orr of Creavery took to the field on 7 June but seems to have taken part only in the action in Randalstown. His summary of the events of that day characterises the conflict as one between Royalists and Republicans:

> The United Irishmen assemble to effect a Revolution and
> thro' off the yoke of military government. A large body of
> people attack Antrim under the command of Henry
> McCracken AG [Adjutant General]. A hard fight ensues. A
> reinforcement comes from Belfast and Blaris Camp and the
> people are repulsed. I am at Randalstown and a number of
> people attack it, beats the Military, disarms them. 2 men
> republicans are killed and 3 royalists. The people repairs to a
> hill in rare of Rev. Hays.[18]

CHAPTER 5 FOOTNOTES

1 The pastor of the Moravian settlement at Gracehill recorded signs of activity in the countryside on 7 June 1798. See: *The 1798 rebellion as recorded in the diaries of Gracehill Moravian Church* produced by two members of Antrim & District Historical Society, John and Enda Cooper for their *Moravian History Magazine*.

2 'Captain' Cook's involvement in deposition of Widow McAllen 8 August 1798 (PRONI D/272/5). Sam Cameron, who was born in Groggan and still lives there, is one of those who keeps alive the location of the Parade Field. Frank Dale, kindly showed me the remains of Warden's Oak.

3 The Rev. Robert Magill's boyhood recollections of June 1798 were published in Young's, *Ulster in '98. Episodes and anecdotes.*

4 Examination of Samuel Orr, 3 July 1798 (Reb. Papers 620/39/14). Court martial of Robert McGowan 30 June 1798 (Reb. Papers 620/2/9/15). For information on the attack on Randalstown see: M'Gee's account in Madden's *Antrim and Down in '98 pages* pp 59-61; Petition on behalf of Thomas Jones Hamilton signed by many of the magistrates in County Antrim (HO/100/110 p242-245); Committal of John French for burning the market house in Randalstown (Reb. Papers 620/47/132); McSkimmin *Annals of Ulster or Ireland fifty years ago* p116.

5 John Dickey from Crumlin, a brother of James Dickey who was executed in Belfast, was most likely one of the Colonels who was reluctant to rise on the 7th June. His court martial (Reb. Papers 620/2/9/1) gives an indication of the chaos this lack of leadership around Crumlin caused. It appears that some United Men entertained the idea of seizing the arms from the soldiers as they passed through Crumlin – after the Battle of Antrim.

6 Information in these paragraphs taken from court martials of Henry and Thomas Anderson (Reb. Papers 620/2/9/15) and John Orr (Reb. Papers 620/17/17).

7 The Orr court martial states that Mary Hunter lived at 'Dormygall'. There is no townland of this name near Antrim, although it might be a corruption of Donegore. The alternative presented here is that it refers to Drumacalliagh, a district, but not a townland on the road to Parkgate as it rises out of Burnside. This place-name, though known to residents there, is not shown on the OS maps.

8 Madden's *Antrim and Down in '98* p 124.

9 A letter of 8 June 1798 from Nugent to Brigadier General Knox in Tyrone states ' there was a pretty general Insurrection in the County of Antrim yesterday morning – I had information at about 6 o'clock on the intention of the insurgents to strike a blow at Antrim and seize upon the magistrates who were to assemble there' (NLI 56/p184).

10 Losses of the 22nd Dragoons in Antrim are detailed in a letter from Lt. Col. William Wollaston to General Lake in Dublin (Reb Papers 620/38/112). It lists 1 Cornet, 1 Quartermaster and 11 'rank and file' as dead. Injured: 1 Lt. Col., 1 Lieut., 1 Cornet and 16-19 rank and file.

11 Madden's *Antrim and Down in '98.* Hope's accounts are on pp 47-53 & 124-127 and Macartney's on pp 53-57.

12 Encounter with the Magheragall Yeoman Cavalry: Smith (1996) *Memories of '98.* p 7

13 Musgrave 1802 *Memoirs of the different rebellions*, p101. Hope, in Madden's *Antrim and Down in '98,* states 'Samuel Orr behaved like a coward at Antrim: His flight caused a party headed by McCracken, who were proceeding to dislodge a party of yeomen in Lord

Massereene's demesne, to take flight' (p50). Earlier, on p48, he stated that 'the party stationed on the west side of the town entered by Bow Lane, but were checked by the destructive fire from the [yeo]men behind the [castle garden] wall. They were forced to retreat at the moment that a body of five hundred men from Connor and Kells, who had taken Randlestown on their march to Antrim [Sam Orr's men?] came to our assistance, and on entering the town, mistook the flying horsemen for a body of the King's troops making a charge, and the retreat of the Bow Lane party for a complete rout.' On page 49 he states that after the battle 'We retreated slowly to Donegore Hill were we expected to find a body of men in reserve, commanded by Samuel Orr, the brother of William Orr' – and so implying that Sam Orr was not supposed to be in Antrim at all. Hope returned to the subject some years later after reading Macartney's views on the Battle of Antrim and repeated his assertion that it was men from Ballyclare who caused the initial panic: 'We were about to attack the horsemen [and, by the same account, yeomen who had re-mained close by the castle walls] when a body of Ballyclare men entered the town by the west end street and Bow Lane [there only is one west end street]. This caused some confusion, and the troops at the market house profitted by it to renew their fire .....The people began to give way ...' (p126). Young (1893) *Ulster in '98*.

14 Reference to McGivern in McSkimmon's *Annals of Ulster*, p123.

15 Nugent's letter to Lake 9 June 1798 (Reb. Papers 620/38/98). Col Durham's report to Major General Nugent 7 June 1798 (Reb. Papers 620/38/85). Recent accounts of the Battle of Antrim can be found in Hall (1998) *A battle lost and won,* Smyth (1984) *The story of Antrim* and Stewart (1995) *The summer soldiers*.

16 James Finlay's evidence in John Orr's court martial (Reb. Papers 620/17/17).

17 Hope in *Antrim and Down in '98* (p49) and Smith's *Memories of '98* (p12). The entries in Magill's names of seat-holders are as follows 'Samuel W. Johnson Sexton was married to Jane McGribben 18 April 1812 by Revd Mr McGarry. He was born 1778, appointed sexton 1823. His father was Arthur Johnson, Townhead, who was killed on the 7th June 1798 by the military and his mother was Jane Campbell who died about the year 1815. Jenny Johnson (daughter of the above Arthur) 7 June 1798 aged 16 years.' These deaths are mentioned by Smith in *Memories of '98* (p5). Madden in *Antrim and Down in '98* (p62) gives a very similar incident but gives the surname as Quin, an unusual name for Antrim.

18 *Diary of an Irish Rebel*. (SRNSW ref: SZ851; Reel 2504)

6
Samuel Orr's losses

Robert Hunter was a Belfast ship-broker and one of the Northern Directory which had resisted forcing rebellion without French assistance. In the wreckage of defeat, he bitterly lamented the actions of the 'violent young men' who had taken the contrary viewpoint, among whom he named Henry Joy McCracken, Henry Munro and Samuel Orr. Hunter had met Orr at least once before the Rebellion, for he and taken him to William Tennent's house in Waring Street. Their purpose was to attend the meeting which elected Robert Simms as Adjutant General of the United Irishmen in Antrim. This was in November 1797 but by then Samuel Orr was already under suspicion for he had been arrested in July 1797 and taken to Belfast, although, apparently not brought to trial. Rev. Arthur Macartney described Orr as 'a man of great muscular strength, noted for his prowess in party feuds, and for his use of the stick, being from his great height, better able to than most men to strike on and over the heads of his opponents'. Even so it is surprising, given his youth, to find Orr at such a senior and secret meeting as the one which took place in Tennent's house. Most likely, the recent execution of his brother had propelled Samuel into a position of leadership at the age of 25.[1]

The day after the Battle of Antrim, Samuel Orr's home at Kilbegs was burned by Col. Clavering's troops and his cattle seized as booty. By this time Samuel Orr had joined Henry Joy McCracken and Jemmy Hope with around 100 followers at Donegore, where they desperately tried to rally their forces. When this failed they moved on to the remote slopes of Slemish mountain. Clavering had been left in command of mid-Antrim and established his head-quarters in Shane's Castle, the home of Lord O'Neill, who was dying from the pike wound he received in Antrim. Clavering's forces were limited, as most of the men who had fought at Antrim had been withdrawn to Belfast in anticipation of dealing with the rising in County Down. Wisely, he made no immediate attempt to seek out the rebel forces but began a policy designed to separate the insurgents from their leaders. Hope maintained that Clavering presented an offer of pardon to all those at Donegore except for four men. One of the four named was Samuel Orr, for whom there was a reward of £100. At this stage no reward was offered for McCracken. In the days that followed, the men on Slemish could only watch as the remnants of United Irish army of County Antrim disintegrated.[2]

On the day after the Battle of Antrim, the rebels around Randalstown attempted to negotiate terms for their surrender, using John Dickey of Hollybrook, Randalstown, as an intermediary. Their bargaining counter was the prisoners they had taken in Randalstown. Clavering promised if these prisoners were released by the dawn of the following day and all weapons surrendered, then he, in return, would release all his prisoners and ensure that 'no-one whatever in this country shall be molested or their property injured'. If they did not comply with these terms, Clavering threatened to 'set fire to and totally destroy Antrim, Randalstown and every town and village and farmhouses with the stock of cattle in this country and put everyone to the sword without any form of tryal whatsoever'! The insurgents in Randalstown endeavoured to take advantage of this offer and cart loads of pikes were delivered from Randalstown to Shane's Castle but the prisoners captured in the town by Samuel Orr's men were not set free. They had been transferred from the camp at Groggan to Ballymena and Clavering used the failure to release them as an excuse to have Randalstown burned by his troops on the morning of Saturday 9 June.

To the north, Ballymena was still occupied by a large rebel force and, as the smoke from Randalstown rose in the summer sky, many of Ballymena's inhabitants began to shift their belongings out of town.

Clavering had accepted two magistrates, Macnevin and McCleverty, to deliver another ultimatum, this time to the rebels in Ballymena. The burning of Randalstown had the desired effect, for by Saturday evening, Ballymena had agreed to surrender, the rebels there would return to their homes and give up their weapons the next day. The rebel leaders were offered the benefit of a trial by their peers, that is a civil trial as opposed to a court martial, but none took this option and it is doubtful if Clavering ever seriously expected that they would.[3]

As soon as Ballymena was secured, Clavering turned his attention to the men on Slemish mountain. Emissaries were dispatched to them stating that they would be attacked unless they dispersed. From Jemmy Hope's and Mary Ann McCracken's accounts it is clear that Slemish was abandoned by Wednesday 13 June, for by that day the rebels, now reduced to less than 30, had moved south across the Glenwherry valley to Big Collin, a hill overlooking Ballyclare and the Sixmilewater valley. From there, according to Hope, they could hear the distant rumble of cannon fire coming from Ballynahinch, some 30 miles away, as General Nugent's artillery battered the County Down rebels into submission. News of this defeat confirmed the futility of continuing the fight in the north and the remnants of McCracken's force spit up, each hoping to find safety as best he could.[4]

Samuel Orr's whereabouts for the next fortnight or so are not known. A notice signed by Clavering and dated 30 June 1798 stated that Samuel Orr and another Antrim leader, Robert Johnston, would no longer benefit from the offer of a civil trial and that 'when apprehended, they will be apprehended as Traitors and Rebels'. This notice was not printed by the *Belfast Newsletter* until 6 July, but by that time Orr had already given himself up. The precise details of Samuel Orr's desertion from his cause are unclear but it is most improbable that he simply surrendered and hoped for the best, at a time when executions were beginning to take place in County Antrim. A more probable scenario is that he began negotiations to agree terms for his surrender which would save his own neck and property. He could draw on the good offices of his brother James Orr, the High Constable at Cranfield, while other lines of communication may have been made through the Redmonds of Thornhill.

What Samuel Orr had on offer was information on the Antrim and Belfast leadership of the United Irishmen. In Belfast, the authorities knew well enough the names of these men but none of their informers would be prepared to reveal themselves in a court of law. In dealing with Orr, the

Government was to trade on his willingness to save his own neck in exchange for evidence which would convict the Belfast leadership, most of whom were under arrest. After the Battles of Antrim and Ballynahinch, it might have been thought that the Government would have resorted to summary executions of these men, but this was not the case. Each prisoner would have the benefit of a trial. To provide the evidence which would convict his prisoners, Pollock, the Crown Solicitor in Belfast, took Samuel Orr's statement on the 3 July 1798.[5]

Pollock had a rather hot temper and may have had something of a personal grudge against the clever Belfast merchants who had for years eluded his grasp. Although Samuel Orr could have testified to the events of the rising, Pollock was much more interested in receiving an account of the meeting in William Tennent's house in Waring Street, for Orr's testimony could convict those who attended it of treason. According to Orr, the meeting elected Robert Simms to the post of General of Antrim in a secret ballot, although after his election, Simms said he thought that Joseph Coulter was the better man. After the election the meeting received a report from a 'strange man from Dublin' to the effect that members of 'the military and other persons who were United Irishmen [were] ready to turn and join against Government in case of insurrection taking place' and that 'the numbers of these persons in Dublin to be innumerable', a boast that was to turn out to be a rather hollow one. Robert Hunter had been transmitting information amongst the various Societies of United Irishmen but no longer wished to continue with this, as he had been in that situation 'so long that it was very dangerous for him to continue longer.'

Samuel Orr's other testimony concerned events in Randalstown and Antrim before and after the Battle of Antrim. For the local historian, these references are tantalisingly brief, but for those he named they could have been damning enough. It is not a surprise that Orr avoided incriminating himself or any of his compatriots from around Randalstown. James Ker from 'near Miss Bristow's' in Antrim had been his contact point for the signal to rise on the day before the Battle of Antrim. Then omitting entirely all mention of events connected with the Battle of Antrim or the attack on Randalstown, Orr continued by revealing the identities of men who had been prepared to continue the struggle after the Battle. One of these was a W. Lather, or Lawther, who also a prisoner and had been 'in arms with a party of fugitive rebels' on the day following the Battle of Antrim. Four more were named in a similar fashion, one of whom was named 'Hoop', who had resolved on 8 June to keep the 'the rebels together and swore they would [kill?] any person who would leave them.' Hoop mentioned is undoubtedly Jemmy Hope, who in elsewhere in the Rebellion Papers is referred to as Hoop.[6]

3 JULY 1798

EXAMINATION ON OATH OF SAMUEL ORR   *REB. PAPERS 620/39/14*

James Ker of _____ near Mifs Bristow's Antrim was the person who on Wed 6th June 1798 gave notice of the intended insurrection. Hill Thompson can prove this.

W.G. Lather [?] a prisoner on Friday 8 June in arms with a party of fugitive Rebels.

One Wilson & _____ Hoop and D. Hamilton on that day made some kind of resolution with a view of keeping the Rebels together and swore they would _____ any person who would leave them. Kilpatrick near Templepatrick which concerned in same.

[I, Samuel Orr] was at meeting five [?] persons in the house of William Tennent in Waring Street Belfast in or about Nov. 1797. The persons present at this meeting were William Tennent, Robert Hunter (who took witness to there) Clotworthy Birnie, Robert Simms, Joseph Coulter (near Colin) Robert _____ of Kells & Young Blackburne of Whitebabbey. A man from Dublin also attended & Robert Hunter and this man read to the meeting certain written papers or reports, the import of which was stating the numbers of military and other persons who were United Irishmen ready to turn out and join against Government in case of Insurrection taking place. Remember they [stated] the numbers of these persons in Dublin to be innumerable.

At this meeting R. Simms then present was elected a General. The mode they elected was by writing names & balloting & the choice fell upon Simms the present, Coulter was the next. After the election, Simms sayd a few word, the import of which was that Coulter was the fittest man but since the meeting elected him he would accept the office.

Witness understood from Robert Hunter that he was in the situation of being employed in carrying reports from one [United Irish] Society to another and said Hunter & strange man from Dublin were the persons who jointly made the report before mentioned. Witness recollects that Hunter sayd at this meeting that he wished the Society would employ another in that situation for he had been so long in it, it was very dangerous for him continue longer.

Witness from the foregoing transactions which he observed at it, knows that the object of the five persons who there met was to assist in exciting rebellion against the Government of this Kingdom. Witness was a United Man & Robert Hunter who took him to the meeting knew him to be as witness believed

SAMUEL ORR
Examined & sworn before me the 3 rd July 1798.

Orr's statement makes no mention of Henry Joy McCracken, but McCracken was not to escape. Four days after the statement, McCracken was captured as he tried to enter Carrickfergus in order to escape on a trading ship moored in Belfast Lough. He was tried in Belfast on 17 July. On the morning of McCracken's court martial, a rumour swept through Belfast that Samuel Orr would be a prosecution witness. Mary Anne McCracken, Henry's sister, records that her brother refused to believe this, but both must have known Samuel Orr had already defected. McCracken's trial was over by mid-afternoon and, at 5 p.m., he was executed in the High Street.[7]

A couple of hours later Pollock scribbled a hasty note to Edward Cooke, the Secretary in Dublin Castle who was pivotal in the Government's management of the situation. It reads:

LETTER FROM JAMES POLLOCK, CROWN SOLICITOR   *REB. PAPERS 620/39/94*
BELFAST TO MR SECRETARY COOKE,
DUBLIN CASTLE
BELFAST, 7 PM 17 JULY 1798

I wrote to you 2 hours ago & aquainted you that Mr Henry Joy McCracken was tryed, convicted and executed this day for leading the rebels at Antrim.
The brother of Orr (The Martyr) prosecuted Hunter, Simms, Coulter and Tennent for being present with other rebels & traitors & electing a General Office to command the Rebels. He will bring the fact home to all but Tenant. He cannot identify him certainly. However I will (I think) fix him in another act of treason before I part.

JAMES POLLOCK

Pollock's eagerness to 'fix' his prisoners did not accord with the policy of the new Lord Lieutenant of Ireland, Lord Cornwallis, which was to conciliate were possible and to put and end to the violent excesses which were disfiguring the quelling of the Rebellion in the south of Ireland. Politically, he wanted to expose the leadership of the United Irishmen, who were under lock and key in Dublin's Newgate prison, and their plans for a democratic republican government linked with France. As Great

Britain was at war with France, revealing these plans would both retrospectively justify the repressive measures the Government had taken since 1793 and render their Whig opponents in London both foolish and naive, for they had long argued that reform rather than revolution would have satisfied the United leadership. After a few Dublin trials and their inevitable executions, most notably of the Sheares brothers, Cornwallis permitted an offer to be made to the ring-leaders of the Rebellion, which would spare their lives in return for a full written account of the United conspiracy. They were not asked to implicate anyone in treason, nor express any remorse. Not surprisingly the prisoners complied and produced a detailed account of the movement's origins, aims and activities leading up to the rising. The Government gleefully rushed to publish this account.

Having spared those who sat at the top table, there was little justification in hanging the only slightly lesser leaders held in Belfast, such as Hunter, Simms and Tennent. They were never prosecuted for their treason, but equally the Government would not set them free in Ireland, where there was every indication that some at least of them would go back to their old ways. An Act of Banishment, exiling these men to countries not at war with Britain was being prepared in early August. By then Pollock was probably utterly frustrated, for as some wags had remarked, why, after slaughtering some 30,000 rebels, should the Government balk at executing 80 or so leaders? Moreover Simms, Tennent and company were unbowed. Pollock summonsed them to ask if they would agree to being exiled. As he noted a letter to Lord Castlereagh; 'All the principal traitors refused it peremptorily'. Pollock still had his prize witness, Samuel Orr, in custody and in the same letter he suggested that the authorities could use Orr's knowledge in their deliberations, in deciding who to banish.

EXTRACT FROM POLLOCK'S LETTER TO   *REB. PAPERS 620/39/205*

LORD CASTLEREAGH, 25 AUG 1798

> Your Lordship shall receive by the next post the list of the prisoners [to be included in the act of Banishment] and the coupon of each man attached, But General Nugent and I think it advisable in the meantime to send up Samuel Orr for the purpose of examining him in the House of Commons and Lords on the Bill of Exile & we think that his evidence will probably justify the Parliament in including Simms, Tennent, Hunter, Coulter and Mr Birnie in the Act.
>
> Your Lordship will please to give orders to have this man carefully sent back here when his business is done in Dublin.

It is not clear if Castlereagh ever made use of Samuel Orr's evidence, but Simms and his colleagues joined the Dublin leadership for three years internment in Fort George, near Inverness. Orr escaped this fate and any other punishment for his involvement in the Rising in Antrim. Jemmy Hope probably never knew that Orr had sworn against him, for if he had, Hope might have heaped even greater scorn on Orr than he did. It was Charles Dickson in his book *Revolt in the North* who first brought to light Orr's statement. Dickson wrote that he felt that Orr's nerve had failed him, which may have been the precise opposite of what happened, but comforted himself with the belief that money had not prompted Orr's actions. In this judgement Dickson may also have been too optimistic, for in the spring of 1799 Samuel Orr dispatched the following letter to Dublin Castle.[8]

KILBEGS 4TH APRIL 1799   *REB. PAPERS 620/46/114*

Sir

Enclosed I send you the amount of my losses I sustained which is estimated very low which I hope you will have the goodness to forward them to the proper place as the Government promised to make up my losses. Your compliance will be much obliged, Your most obedient & humble servant

SAML. ORR.

Orr obviously expected to be compensated for the losses incurred when his home was burned. This expectation can only be understood in the light of his evidence given the previous July. Accompanying the letter were five pages of inventories. Three concerned the rebuilding of the house and farm buildings at Kilbegs plus the rebuilding costs of another house at Duneane, located between Toomebridge and Randalstown. The remainder listed the extensive furniture and farm implements lost when Kilbegs was burned and, we may suppose, looted. The list of furniture, with its mahogany tables and chairs, is an eloquent testimony to the wealth that some County Antrim farmers had accumulated at the end of the eighteenth century. The total claimed was a not inconsiderable sum of £866 18s 3d. Orr had obtained the signature of Jackson Clarke, the magistrate of the Steeple, Antrim, as to the account's veracity. The records do not state whether the Government ever 'made up' Samuel Orr's losses. One can only hope that they did not.[9]

CHAPTER 6 FOOTNOTES

1 Robert Hunter's account of the events in the North as told to an informer (Reb. Papers 620/7/74/5). Samuel Orr's statement in Reb. Papers 620/39/14. Report of the arrest of Sam Orr in *The Times* 26 July 1797 as reprinted in Killen, J. (1997) *The decade of the United Irishmen. Contemporary accounts 1791-1801*, p103. Macartney's description in Madden's *Antrim and Down in '98,* p54.

2 Major General Nugent's letter of 9th June 1798 to Lord Castlereagh, states 'Samuel Orr, brother to the man who was hanged at Carrickfergus headed the Rebels at the attack on the troops at Antrim on the 7th . Yesterday evening his house was most completely burnt and his cattle brought in.' (Reb. Papers 620/38/98). Madden's *Antrim and Down in '98*, p 50-53.

3 For Clavering's proclamations see Appendix I.

4 Madden *op. cit.*, p 52.

5 Samuel Orr's statement (Reb. Papers 620/39/14).

6 e.g. Robert Henry's statement (Reb. Papers 620/47/100) mentions 'James Hoop of the Parish of Templepatrick muslin weaver'. Dickson (1960) *Revolt in the North* reprinted parts of Samuel Orr's statement but mis-transcribes Hope as Hoey (pp174-175).

7 Madden *op. cit*, pp 66-73.

8 Dickson (1960) p174.

9 Sam Orr's losses are reprinted as Appendix II. This is the second occasion in the story of the Orrs when Jackson Clarke appears, each time favouring an Orr. It is perhaps a coincidence, but Malcomson's (1972) chronicle of *The extraordinary career of the 2nd Earl of Massereene, 1743-1805* (p101) reprints Massereene's description of Clarke as a 'soap boiler' and as one of the 'Heirarchs of the United bands'.

7
That John Orr is a
Treator and a Rebel

William Orr of Creavery summed up the aftermath of the Battle of Antrim as follows: 'The people are in the fields. The yeomen plunder and rack the country indiscriminately'. The yeomanry companies of County Antrim have indeed taken much of the blame for the pillage which took place, although the Monaghan Militia were not shy in this regard. John Dickey of Crumlin complained that Edward Wakefield, Captain of the Ballinderry Yeoman Cavalry, had 'pulled down houses which he sold to be carried off, consisting of the roofes, lofts, doors etc. etc and also seized — all the property — which he yet retains'. In a few cases, these attacks were accompanied by killings, the most notorious of which was when Thomas Hamilton Jones of the Toome Yeoman Cavalry killed David Neill at Moneyglass. Neill had taken part in the attack on the Market House in Randalstown and, when Jones was being taken prisoner, Neill had to be restrained from piking him. As well as Samuel Orr's home at Kilbegs, the homes of John Orr at The Folly, his son Samuel Orr at Harp Hall and Widow William Orr at Farranshane were all burnt. While the yeomen

Harp Hall stands today as ruins. The house was rebuilt after 1798 and was the home of Sam Orr, the son of John Orr of The Folly.

looted her house before torching it, Mrs Orr hid in the fields of neighbouring Rathbeg with her six children, including Wilhelmina, who had only been born in April 1798.[1]

Clavering's proclamation of a £100 reward for the arrest of Samuel Orr also named John Orr and William Orr. The latter must have been the watchmaker from Creavery, but the identity of John Orr is more problematic as it could have been either William's brother or his Uncle John of The Folly. These three were aware that they were wanted men, for they kept out of sight in the weeks that followed. John Orr of The Folly remained in hiding until August and his neighbour, James Finlay, thought that Orr had been killed during the Battle of Antrim. Many from County Antrim contrived to flee to the USA by an escape route which was soon established with the connivance of at least two magistrates. John Orr of Creavery availed of this to flee to America on 15 July 1798. He was 29 years old. [2]

On the 17 July, the day of McCracken's execution, a countrywide amnesty was introduced covering all who had laid down their arms, except for named leaders and those insurgents accused of capital crimes such as murder. For County Antrim, the names of twenty-one men were published in the *Belfast Newsletter* of 23 July, each of whom had a reward of 50 guineas for his capture. Of all the Antrim Orrs, only John Orr of The Folly was included in this list and so William Orr of Creavery, who was still in hiding, was free to return to his home. After waiting a week, perhaps to test the sincerity of the government, William returned to his ruined home with his mother and sister, Nancy. In the absence of his brother, William had plenty to occupy him for the house had to be rebuilt and, of equal importance, the harvest had to taken in. For this, there was the assistance of neighbours but one of these was an army deserter, by the name of McCammon or McCallom who was living under an assumed name of Mayse. This man was to leave before the harvest was completed, with William Orr accusing him of stealing clothing, a quarrel which was to have serious repercussions for William Orr in the following year.[3]

His inclusion in the list of 'Leaders and Principal Agitators in the Rebellion' had provided John Orr of the Folly with rather stark alternatives: He could remain in hiding with the probability of execution if captured and with the risk that anyone found harbouring him would also suffer this fate. Or he could follow his nephew to America and start a new life there, but this would not be easy given his age. Alternatively John Orr could surrender and attempt to refute the charges against him in court or, at the least, hope to gain some degree of clemency by surrendering voluntarily. By mid-August John Orr had re-appeared in his community, so scotching the persistent rumours that he was dead. Using one of his sons as a go-between, he approached the Rev. Macartney as to the best terms of his surrender but Macartney refused to mediate, telling Orr to surrender direct to the military. Orr must have dreaded this advice for he would have fancied his chances with a civil jury of his peers above that of a military court-martial. Nevertheless, the prospect of life on the run must have been unattractive for he gave himself up to the military. On 15 November 1798, a court martial began in Belfast to try John Orr as a 'treator and a rebel'.[4] (The transcript of his trial is printed in Appendix III).

John Orr faced a bench of five officers: four captains and the president, Major Anderton of the Lancashire Light Dragoons. The prosecutor was a junior officer, Lieut. Ffolliot Whiteway. The trial transcript shows the prosecution case depending on proving that John Orr had been a leader of the United Irishmen at the Battle of Antrim. His presence in the insurgent ranks at Antrim was not disputed and both defence and prosecution witnesses admitted that they too had been under arms in Antrim. Only by establishing John Orr as a leader would he be found guilty of the charge of treason – for which the penalty was death. The trial provides vignettes as to the disorganisation of the Rebels on the morning of the Battle of Antrim, and elements of perhaps unintentional humour.

John English, whom Orr had tried to dissuade from entering Antrim on the day of the battle, gave his testimony against John Orr. James Finlay appeared as a defence witness and claimed to have marched into Antrim with Orr on his right hand but stated that Orr held only the rank of a private soldier. Under cross-examination, Finlay admitted that he fled down an entry from the main street in Antrim and went home when the first cannon was fired. He could not swear that Orr had not been in charge at some later time in the Battle. Also giving evidence was Mary Hunter, whose sons Orr had attempted to enlist, and Henry Anderson. While both were willing to give evidence of a factual nature, they would not say that John Orr, their neighbour, was a leader. Anderson had been court-martialed with a Thomas Anderson in Antrim in late June, on the evidence of Henry O'Hara. These Antrim court martials were desultory affairs for it was clear that both Andersons had only a minimal involvement in the fighting but each had implicated a man named Orr who had forced them to turn out. When cross-examined in John Orr's court martial, Henry Anderson claimed not to know if Orr had any command and, attempting to soften his evidence, asserted he had only joined the rebel forces that day when forced to do so by another man. Mary Hunter was also circumspect, refusing to swear that the John Orr in the dock was the man who had come looking for her sons – she claimed to have been only told his name was John Orr. Again an unlikely scenario, given that she lived not far from The Folly.[5]

The prosecution case rested on the evidence of Henry O'Hara who was the first witness. O'Hara had already given evidence not only against the Andersons but also against John Storey, one of the leaders during the Battle of Antrim, albeit not a very effective one. The testimony of O'Hara had been sufficient to condemn Storey to the gallows where he died on 5 July 1798. John Storey had been a printer on the *Northern Star* in Belfast but he would have been known to John Orr, for the Storey family was from Islandbawn, not far from The Folly. The sight of O'Hara beginning to give evidence must have been a chilling one to John Orr. His evidence was also damning; Orr was in charge of a party of 20 to 30 men armed with guns pitch forks and pikes. He had been making pikes the night before the Battle and appeared to be in command as he issued threats to burn the houses of those who would not join him. As the rebel column approached Antrim, Orr was stated to have given an order that the young men were to go to the front. O'Hara could not be shaken from his account and was able to turn cross-examination to the prosecution's advantage. When questioned about an encounter with an 'orderly man', whom John Orr was keen to argue was directing events before the Battle, O'Hara's reply emphasised the importance of Orr, by noting that the orderly man had implied that the rebel army would not march from Templepatrick to Antrim without the arrival of John Orr in person.

Against this evidence, Finlay claimed Orr had been asked to take command in Templepatrick but had refused, while James Johnston and Robert Kirk were willing to contradict O'Hara's contention that Orr had been in command in Antrim. None of them had seen Orr force anyone into the Insurgent ranks. All these men were closely cross-examined by Whiteway and their integrity questioned. Finlay admitted to have taken the Oath of Allegiance before the Battle of Antrim and none had taken the Oath of Allegiance since the Rising. Neither Finlay nor Johnston could offer any explanation other than a 'fear of being taken up' as to why John Orr would have remained in hiding after the proclamation of amnesty.[6]

O'Hara's evidence was crucial. Col. Sinclare of the 22nd Light Dragoons denied repeated accusations that O'Hara was being paid for his evidence. On the third and final day of the trial the Rev. Macartney testified that O'Hara had given evidence against 'many persons who were concerned in the Rebellion' and considered that O'Hara's testimony was 'worthy of belief in a Court of Justice'. That completed the evidence. The papers of the trial do not state how long the bench of five officers took to consider the evidence, but their verdict was clear. John Orr was guilty of the crimes laid to his charge and was sentenced 'to be hanged by the neck until he is dead at such time and place as Major General Goldie shall be pleased to appoint.'

CHAPTER 7 FOOTNOTES

1 John Dickey's petition from New Geneva (SPP 528); Petition on behalf of Thomas Jones Hamilton signed by many of the magistrates in County Antrim (HO/100/110 p242-245). Smith (1888) *Historical gleanings in Antrim and neighbourhood,* (p23) mentions that Farranshane and The Folly were burned, although the latter is given as the home of James Orr, the son of John Orr. Bigger in *Remember Orr* (p14) adds Harp Hall to the list of houses which were burnt.

2 Hope in Madden, *Antrim and Down in '98* (p50) states that £100 was offered by Clavering for William, John and Samuel Orr as well as Robert Johnstone. According to Hope, John Orr escaped from Islandmagee to America. In his diary William Orr simply states 'July 15th 1798 Brother escapes to America'. (In: *Diary of an Irish rebel.* SRNSW ref:SZ 851; Reel 2504).

3 Also in the *Diary* is the subsequent entry: 'Aug 1st 1798. I return to brother's house with mother and sister. Begin to rebuild the burned houses and reaps the harvest. A dizerter of the name of McCammon other wise Maise employed at harvest. He runs away and steals my clothes.'

4 Court martial of John Orr (Reb. Papers 620/17/17).

5 Court martials of Thomas and Henry Anderson in Antrim 25 June 1798 (Reb. Papers 620/2/9/15). Both were only sentenced to find securities for their future good behaviour. Also tried, and acquitted after no evidence was produced, at this court martial was David McQuillan, one of William Orr's neighbours. Robert Magill visited both Thomas Anderson and David McQuillan on 31 July 1827. He recorded in his *Names of seat holders* that McQuillan died on 19 Sept. 1833 aged 77.

6 James Finlay. Readers of *Dear Uncle* (Foy, 1989) may remember references to James Finlay by James Kerr in his letters to his uncles in Newpark (just up the Greystone road from The Folly) in the 1840s: 'Old Jamie Finlay, is he still able to trudge up and down the road, may he long do so' (p97). Finlay lived at Finlay's Forth, a rath beside The Folly and, according to Magill's *Names of seatholders,* was a Covenanter.

8
The Flogging Committees

When she considered the fortunes of the Orrs around Antrim, Mrs Elizabeth Orr would have had little to celebrate as 1799 dawned. Their homes at Kilbegs, Farranshane, The Folly and Harp Hall, as well as her own at Creavery, had been looted and burnt. Isabella Orr had returned to her house at Farranshane and begun to put it to rights, but life as a widow with six children to rear and a farm to run was not going to be easy. She would have the help of John Orr's son Samuel, from neighbouring Harp Hall, but his house had also been burnt and he was father to three very young children. Over at Kilbegs, Eliza's other nephew Samuel was in disgrace, but at least he was there to provide for his four young children. Not so for her brother-in-law John of The Folly, but his children were grown-up and well able to fend for themselves. Although he still lay in a prison cell in Belfast, John was at least alive as his death sentence had not been confirmed by Lord Cornwallis. Indeed how they could they hang him when, in truth, much greater United men had escaped the hangman's noose?[1]

Eliza's own lot cannot have brought her any great comfort. True her house had been rendered habitable, but her worries must have centred on John and William. Was John safe in America? – Perhaps he would come home if things settled down, for she could not run the farm herself. True, William was at home but his trade was watch-making. But would things settle down? For the cause for which her sons had risen for in 1798 did not die in Antrim on 7 June 1798. William was meeting with men who would be happy to see the embers of rebellion fanned back into flame. William Orr summarised the winter of 1798-99 as follows: 'Parties of proclaimed U.I. men assemble in the nights, takes arms from Loyalists and punish informers.'[2]

Defeat in Antrim had so unnerved the United Irishmen that the army had no need to engage them again in County Antrim. As a result the great majority of United men would have had no first-hand experience of the terror of battle. But for some of these men, the scale of the uprising, with perhaps over ten thousand men turning out, must have suggested that victory could yet be won, a hope buoyed up by continuing rumours of a fresh French expedition. Although most of the Belfast based leadership had been arrested, comparatively few of the country leadership in Antrim had been arrested and still fewer executed. For the loyalists in County Antrim, William Orr was another conspirator who had been allowed to escape his just deserts. Young and hot-blooded, these men were now free to travel the lanes and byways of Antrim, meeting together on market days in the back rooms of inns such as that of John Moore's in Ballymena. For both loyalist and rebel, the policy of conciliation pursued since July 1798 may have been interpreted as weakness, encouraging those predisposed to be disloyal while unnerving the loyalist.[3]

Those who wished to continue the quarrel would have known that a United Irish command had been re-established in Dublin. Robert Henry, a schoolteacher of Connor, had been proclaimed in July 1798 but not captured until mid-1799. The statement he gave then claimed that James Hope had brought a plan of re-organisation from United Irishmen's National Committee to a County Antrim meeting held in March 1799. The county was expected to raise twelve regiments of 1000 men, each headed by a colonel who was to be under the command of three generals for the county. The National Committee would appoint the generals, showing a desire to centralise control in comparison to the devolved power structure that characterised the local leadership of the United Irishmen before the Rising.[4]

Rumours of a fresh rising were rife, leaving the Moravian community at Gracehill in fear of retribution from their neighbours, for the Moravian policy was to support the Government. Moravian pastors were expected to keep a dairy recording secular and religious life and the Gracehill pastor, John Steinhauser, kept a diary throughout 1798 and 1799. A native of Estonia, Steinhauser recorded that a second insurrection was expected to break out on Christmas Eve 1798 and that his congregation sought refuge in great numbers at the Christmas Eve service. A more tangible form of United activity soon followed on the 30 December 1798 with the houghing of a soldier, John Forsythe, in Ballymena, the victim being maimed by cutting his Achilles' tendons. This outrage brought an offer of a reward in the *Belfast Newsletter* but no-one in Ballymena, other than two magistrates, felt confident enough of their safety to put his name to a reward for the capture of those who had crippled Private Forsythe. At the same time, the *Newsletter* carried declarations of loyalty from the Roman Catholic Parishes of north Antrim but from the Presbyterian congregations in the heart-lands of mid-Antrim there was only a sullen silence.[5]

Heavy snow-falls in January 1799 hampered troop movements in the countryside and the military gave orders for the roads to be cleared. Pastor Steinhauser recorded that this 'was done cheerfully and expeditiously' in Gracehill, but in the neighbouring village of Ahoghill, the citizens would not clear the roads until forced to do so by soldiers from Ballymena. With the snow clearing both soldiers and United men could begin to move more freely and, from late January to May, the *Belfast Newsletter* recorded a litany of robberies and floggings. The greater number of these, by far, emanated from County Antrim. The middle of the county was the most virulent area, with the insurrection stretching up the valley of the River Main and along the Kells, Braid and Clough rivers. Initially, there were frequent reports from along the Six Mile Water valley but these tailed off as spring gave way to summer in 1799. By comparison the areas north of Cloughmills and in the Glens of Antrim seemed to have been free of, what the Rev. Hudson, a Portglenone magistrate, called 'the flogging committees'.[6]

William Orr described the activities of the resurgent United men as the punishment of informers and the seizure of arms. In Clough a man was reported to have had 'half his tongue cut out', but mostly the nocturnal visitors contented themselves with flogging their victims, although these too could be brutal in the extreme. Among those who suffered retribution was Henry O'Hara, who had given evidence against John Orr and John Storey. In April, the *Newsletter* reported that he had been taken from his house and flogged so severely that he was not expected to live. The victims of two other floggings were also reported as not being expected to recover from their injuries, one from just outside Ballymena at Crebilly and the other from a little further away in Kells. The Kells incident on 24 April 1799 resulted in the death of Andrew Swann. On that night Swann and William Dobbs were dragged from their houses by men with blackened faces and tied to a tree. The flogging committee was led by John Egleson and they were sufficiently numerous for different individuals to each administer 25 lashes until Swann had received 500 in total. At times the flogging was not severe enough for Egleson, as Swann related how Egleson encouraged one flogger to 'strike harder, cut him lower, hit him on the hips, it is no flogging at all.' Swann lingered on for almost two weeks after this ordeal and implicated both Egleson and another man, Robert McDonnell. These two denied their involvement, produced alibis, and William Dobbs, the other man flogged, was unable or refused to identify either Egleson or McDonnel. Despite this, both were found guilty on the dead man's evidence but only Egleson was executed in Ballymena on 17 June 1799.[7]

Informers were not the only ones who suffered. Andrew M'Dowal was a tailor by trade, who lived at the Grange, beside Groggan Mountain. On a night of a full moon in April 1799, M'Dowal's house was visited by a party headed by George Dixon, who had been one of the leaders when Randalstown was captured by the rebels. Since then Dixon had gained further fame and notoriety and was known by his *nomme de guerre* of General Holt. When the nocturnal visitors burst into M'Dowal's cottage, they found him hiding under a bed from where he was dragged into the kitchen and told to strip. Dixon then tied M'Dowal's hands while inquiring if he could dance? M'Dowal replied that he 'was not very good at it'. To this, Dixon said he should try, for he was a dancing master from France come to teach a Loyalist to dance. Dixon then asked his companions what was M'Dowal's crime? The reply was burning houses, suggesting that M'Dowal was a yeoman. M'Dowal was then whipped with a pair of tawse until he fainted. Dixon revived him with water and was alleged to have spoken lightly of the fainting. When some of the crowd threatened to smash the windows of the house, Dixon forbade this, threatening to punish anyone who damaged any part of the house. He must have been confident of his authority, for he promised M'Dowal one guinea for every pane of glass in the house which was broken. This, and other evidence concerning Dixon's activities, were sufficient to convict him and he was hanged in Belfast on 16 June 1799. The *Newsletter* described him as a strong well-built man, about 30 years of age, who would not allow his head to be covered at his execution.[8]

The other and more pressing activity of the United Irishmen in 1799 was to re-arm. After the Battle of Antrim it must have been painfully obvious that pikes and pitchforks were of limited utility against the fire-power of the military. There is evidence that United Men were manufacturing gunpowder in 1799, as Dr Patrick of Ballymena was alleged to have provided the materials for making gunpowder to 'the Boyds of Dungall' in February 1799. Making good quality gunpowder required a finely ground product, and James Thompson, an apothecary in Ballymena, also supplied the Boyds with a sieve to 'sift gunpowder'. Arms were a bigger problem, as most of the United guns had been surrendered under the terms of the amnesty of June 1798. Clavering's command to hand in arms covered those held by loyalist families and Robert Magill recorded his father's sadness at having to surrender a sword that an ancestor had at the Battle of the Boyne. By the winter of 1798-99 there were, therefore, comparatively few weapons in the countryside and most of those were in hands of elements hostile to the United Irishmen: the magistrates, yeomanry and, of course, the military.[9]

In December 1798, soldiers of the Tay Fencibles regiment were marching to Kilrea, but three of their number, who were unwell, had unwisely been allowed to fall behind the main marching body and following them was a sergeant. These stragglers were attacked by George Dixon and a party of men near the Grange and, although no serious injury was done to the soldiers, some of their weapons were seized. However soldiers did not often present themselves as such easy targets and General Green in Ballymena soon took steps to recover arms which were vulnerable to seizure. The Gracehill Moravians had been supplied with muskets for their defence in July 1798, but they were ordered to return these to the army on 11 January 1799. Moravians, as noted before, trod a delicate path between their instincts, which were towards loyalty and support for the military, and the inclinations of many of their neighbours around Ahoghill, who were of a decidedly opposite tendency. The Moravian diary states, without comment, that the order to return arms was complied with, but it is likely that Pastor Steinhauser was alarmed that news of this act of co-operation would bring retribution upon the heads of his congregation – especially since it rendered them defenceless. This may have been the motive behind a rather different account of the hand-over which appeared in the *Newsletter* on the 15 January 1799; 'We hear from Ballykennedy

[Gracehill] that on Wednesday last, two men habited as light dragoons went to the Moravian Society there and demanded the arms with which that Society had been entrusted for their protection for the use of the Government. Diligent search had been made for these villains but hitherto in vain'.[10]

The quest for arms led to attacks on magistrates, constables and yeomanry. At the beginning of February 1799, Crebilly House, the home of the Rev. William McCleverty, was attacked and 'striped' of arms. The raiders were disappointed not to find McCleverty at home and left vowing that he would not have lived 30 minutes if he had been there as he had been active in putting a number of their friends to death. McCleverty was a magistrate who had been taken prisoner in Ballymena the previous June. He had been injured then when he was knocked from his horse and for this crime two brothers called Montgomery were executed in Ballymena. His injuries then did not seem so serious, for he had subsequently acted as an intermediary in the negotiations between Clavering and the rebels in Ballymena. But, in February 1799, McCleverty was in Bath and a day or so after his house was raided, it was stated that he had died from wounds he had received in June 1798.[11]

Another magistrate, Squire Agnew of Kilwaughter Castle, near Larne, had also taken the precaution of moving to Bath in the winter of 1798-9 when his house was raided. Agnew had been on good terms with the rebels and acted as a go-between the United forces camped at Glenarm and the military. After the rebellion he had assisted in facilitating the escape of some of them to America. Not surprisingly, Agnew was suspected by loyalists as being rather too friendly and sympathetic to the rebels and his resignation from the command of the local yeomanry drew adverse and ironic comment in a notice in the *Newsletter*: 'Mr Agnew being too humble for an officer and too great to fall to the ranks, he may retire on that rank that is best suited to his feelings, and indulge himself in the satisfaction arising from his exertions through life in support of the Government and the Constitution that gave him protection'.[12]

While magistrates could decamp to places of safety, barony high-constables and their sub-constables were not so fortunate. During February 1799, and within a mere five miles of the newly built army barracks in Ballymena, arms were seized from the homes of constables in Broughshane, Ahoghill and Killymurris. On each occasion the raiders searched other houses for arms and operated in comparatively large numbers and with impunity in terms of local resistance. The *Newsletter* report of the raid on

Samuel Moore's home in Broughshane recorded that 'after searching several respectable houses, [the raiders] fired a gun and walked off'. Again the newspaper noted that the raiders' singleness of purpose – 'It is worthy of observation that they took nothing but arms'. Also perhaps worthy of observation is that, although the Randalstown district was specifically singled out as an area where whipping was most prevalent, there were no reports of any arms taken from the high constable there, James Orr of Cranfield.[13]

At the end of February 1799, the homes of two yeomen at Straid named Junkin and McGolpin were attacked and their guns taken. In March it was reported that the homes of the Glenarm yeomanry had been burned. Close to Antrim, a major raiding expedition was reported at the Milltown, next to Samuel Orr's home at Kilbegs on 2 February. The attacks took place at around 9 p.m. and the group was estimated to be about 40 in number. As elsewhere, the aim was to seize arms but one person was killed and others injured. The first report in the *Newsletter* gave the name of the man killed 'by these ruffians' as Hollis, from which it would be concluded that Hollis was on the side of the loyal inhabitants. Subsequent notices offering rewards for the arrest of the Milltown attackers specifically mentions that a resident was robbed and killed.[14]

There was a widespread expectation that the French would soon arrive. Leonard McNally alias JW, the United Irish lawyer but also the prince of the Government's informers, wrote in May 1799 'an invasion is expected by my friends and the [Government] force here [County Antrim] I don't conceive adequate to the great body of disaffected that will doubtless rise to their assistance'. Lieutenant Murphy of the Toome Yeoman Cavalry was alternatively begging Dublin Castle to tell him the truth as to the arrival of a French invasion and then warning Dublin as to the imminent nature of their arrival. The Rev. Cupples, a Lisburn magistrate, wrote in mid-March 1799 to Dublin that 'Things are worse now than at this time last year. The United Irishmen are preparing themselves to receive aid from France'. The prospect of a French invasion and the nightly attempts by the United Irishmen to seize arms unnerved loyalists. At the end of February there was a report that a 'very liberal collection' had been made for the purpose of fortifying the Market House in Antrim into a 'place of strength' which would afford the inhabitants with 'a safe refuge'. In Ballymena the garrison was on the alert and probably on edge when, on a night in early March, a sentinel thought he spied a number of men in a field at the edge of the town. A general alarm was raised, 'the drums beat to arms, the whole troops in the town collected, the inhabitants were commanded to clap lights in their windows and keep indoors'.[15]

General Nugent, who was still in command of the North, was rebuffed in February 1799 when he asked Dublin to sanction the use of court martials in County Antrim. However, faced with the rising tide of terror in the countryside, the policy of relying on ordinary courts became untenable. On 12 March 1799 the Government made a decisive move to regain the initiative by re-establishing martial law in County Antrim. A curfew was enforced between one hour after sunset and sunrise and no cars were to pass through Antrim town on Sundays except 'they are bringing people to church'. Strangers were required to identify themselves and lists of inhabitants were to be posted on doors of each house. Pastor Steinhauser recorded that on the evening of 12 March that 'In consequence [of the new regulations] we had a very quiet evening, as none of the Market men who frequent our Inn stayed longer than till 8 o'clock'. Three days later Steinhauser noted that 'two of our Single Sisters, Gore, living in a cottage in the country, had their windows broken for obeying the Commanding Officer's orders by having their names struck up on their door.' Blacksmiths and publicans could only operate if they possessed a licence and the magistrates were publicly entreated to make the strictest enquiry into the characters of persons to whom they granted licences. Two magistrates could now commit anyone to gaol who they suspected of being involved in insurrection without the necessity of a trial. Those, for whom firm evidence of wrongdoing could be produced, faced the prospect of a court martial.[16]

The mere introduction of martial law by no means stopped the activities of the flogging committees and they continued throughout March and April. Henry O'Hara's flogging took place in early April along with attacks in the parishes of Dunaghy and Glenwhirry. But reports of arrests became more frequent. On the evening of 16 April 1799, the Rev. George Macartney rode out of Antrim with an escort of yeomanry and soldiers of the 22nd Dragoons to arrest United Irishmen living in townlands to the north of the town: Dunsilly, Kilgavanagh and Creavery. He did not arrive at William Orr's house in Creavery until midnight whereupon Orr was taken from his bed and conveyed to the Antrim Guardhouse. Others arrested on that night included Edward McGrogan, William, Francis and Samuel Agnew and John Kennedy. No resistance was offered and one of their quarry, Andrew Atcheson, who was not found that night, later gave himself up voluntarily.[17]

From Antrim the prisoners were taken to Belfast where their arrival prompted a brief report in the *Newsletter* of 30 April 1799:

'On Saturday last the following prisoners were brought in and lodged in the Provo[s]t Prison by a party of horse and yeoman infantry, from Antrim under the command of Lieutenant Murphy: William Orr (alias Col. Green), of Creavery; Edward McGrogan of Dunsilly; William Agnew of Crosscanon [Crosskennon]; John Montgomery of Trench [Rathmore]; John Brown Cloughmills, Michael O'Kean Kenmore; James Gardner, Brade; and Samuel Martin Dickie taken in arms near Doagh.'

In Belfast William Orr claimed he was not interrogated, but that a panel of three officers, Majors Seddon, Fox and McCoy, acting as magistrates, applied themselves to persuade the others arrested to implicate Orr. These neighbours were threatened with floggings and hanging if they would not co-operate but, when they refused to submit to these threats, rewards were substituted. William Orr claimed that Andrew Atcheson refused '500 guineas, besides his liberty and other valuable emoluments' if he would only testify. When his court martial began on the 9 May 1799, William Orr faced a long charge list: treason & rebellion, aiding and assisting in taking up arms, making ball cartridges and being out of his house after sunset and before sunrise. All those arrested with Orr had refused to give evidence but the Crown was able to produce another neighbour as their star witness: James Mayse, the man William Orr had accused of stealing his clothes at Creavery in the previous autumn.[17]

The evidence of Mayse was that he had seen William Orr and John Kennedy, one of those arrested, making ball cartridges in a barn and garden. More seriously, Orr was the leader of a party which had been seizing arms from houses – referred to in the charge list as 'taking up arms'. Orr was accused of raiding three houses: Squire Agnew's at Kilwaughter, James Ferguson's of Whitepark near Doagh and Williamson's of Freemanstown in the hills above Parkgate. On returning from this raid in an intoxicated state Orr was alleged to have told Mayse of the houses attacked and the arms stolen. Orr was wearing a green jacket and described himself as Colonel Green and was accompanied by another called Colonel Holt – George Dixon, who was to stand trial after William Orr. There was only the evidence of Mayse to implicate Orr, for no-one in the houses which were raided could identify Orr as one of the robbers.

For his defence, Orr called two witnesses, each of whom agreed that the character of Mayse was 'a very bad one'. In addition he prepared a written statement of his defence, reproduced here, which he presented to the court. The *Belfast Newsletter's* court martial reports make no reference to defence counsel – indeed the whole point of such trials was to do way with such niceties – what Castlereagh described as the 'Clerking Jurisdiction'. Rather the accused were left to present their defence as best they could. Against this, Orr's statement is cogently argued with better grammar than found in either his notes or letters which have survived, suggesting he had a lawyer to help him draft his statement either during an interval in the trial, or even before it.

Orr's statement emphasised the impossibility of proving a negative, and asked the court to consider the evidence of Mayse, his manners, motives for giving it and its inconsistencies. After the Battle of Antrim, Mayse claimed that Orr had 'showed him a dryness', for Mayse had not turned out that day, yet after a night of 'housebreaking and robbery, I [Orr] called him out of bed to tell what I had done'. Mayse swore there was snow on the ground but both Ferguson and Agnew's servant swore there was no snow on the night they were robbed. The evidence of those robbed and the advertisement placed by Agnew in the *Newsletter* offering a reward indicated that that the robberies were committed on three different nights yet Mayse's testimony was that Orr had claimed all three on a single night. Mayse swore he saw Orr at dusk on the evening of the robberies, yet the farthest house, Agnew Castle, was robbed only a couple of hours later, at a distance of 20 miles away from Creavery.

The remainder of Orr's statement is made up by a description of his own circumstances and his innocence of any involvement in the United Irishmen. Not surprisingly, no mention is made of his being in Randalstown on 7 June 1798 or that Major Seddon had specifically asked to see William Orr when he burnt his house. While professing confidence that he would be acquitted, he nevertheless offered to go to America. His confidence was misplaced for William Orr was found guilty and was sentenced to serve the King of Prussia.

STATEMENT OF WILLIAM ORR   *PRONI T/1956/3*

Mr President

The crimes of which I am charged are many and the evidence to support them rests entirely on one man, and from the manner in which he has delivered his evidence, stating it all to be in conversation with myself and persons whom he implicates equally, It is impossible I can be prepared with evidence to disprove it – I must therefore humbly submit to the Court that the principal part of my defence rests upon their humane interposition in considering the character of the witness, the manner of delivering his evidence, his motives for giving it, and their [sic] comparing his evidence with that given by the witnesses Ferguson, Williamson and Mr Agnew's servant, to judge if it was possible for me to have had a part in the crimes charged within the time positively sworn to by the witness Mayse – I beg leave to trouble the court with an observation or two on the evidence – Mayse swears the time to be 6 or 8 weeks ago and that I told him Ferguson, Williamson and Agnew Castle were robbed on the same night and between dusk in the evening and day break, which I compute to be at that season only a space of 9 hours- The distance from my mother's house to Agnew Castle was admitted to be 17 miles in a direct line, so that to commit the robberies charged I must have travelled 34 miles in the space of 9 hours, gone to three different houses which must occupy some part of the time – The same witness swears I could have shot him at all times after the 7th June for not turning out on that day, or to use his more direct words (I showed him a dryness) and notwithstanding I on the morning of my return from house breaking and robbery, I called him out of bed as a confidential person to tell him what I had done, yet he can give no account of what was done with the arms which he saw – He swears there was snow on the ground, Ferguson swears there was none when he was robbed, and Agnew's servant swears there was none when his master was robbed. And from the evidence of Ferguson, Williamson and Mr Agnew's servant may be collected that the three robberys [sic] charged were committed on three different nights, Mayse saw me at dusk in the evening and Agnew Castle was robbed at half past 8 in the evening 17 miles off!

I beg leave to refer the Court, to the Newspaper advertizing Mr Agnew's robbery and stating it to have been committed 21st of February

I fear to trespass too much on the time of the Court and shall conclude with a brief account of myself – I was bred to the trade of watchmaker, and worked in Dublin until the beginning of the year 1797, when I came home on my father's death to reside with my mother and brother. On my arrival I found that several of my relatives had been charged with some of the crimes which then disgraced the country, And I profitted by the melancholy examples I saw before me and studiously avoided entering into any Society or Schemes whatsoever, Shortly after my Mother's house was destroyed by the military on account of my brother being suspected of being concerned in the insurrection, and I then was obliged to seek a home elsewhere – The opprobrium brought on my family and the vengeance which seems to follow them at home added to the loss of what property I had made me form a resolution of going to America to avoid suspicion and strive to better my fortune, and I would even now have carried my intentions into effect were it not for my present unhappy situation, and though from the Honor [sic] and humanity of this Court I have every reason to hope for an honorable acquittal after hearing evidence on my part, Yet I beg leave to propose to the Court that I am ready to depart to America at my own expense the first ship that offers, and in the mean time to give ample security for the performance of this my engagement should this honorable Court be graciously pleased to accept of my proposal.

In receiving his sentence Orr was fortunate, for his alleged fellow Colonel, George Dixon, who was tried immediately after him, also for treason and rebellion, was executed. That William Orr escaped this fate may reflect the flimsy and flawed nature of the evidence against him. The prime purpose of the trial was to remove from circulation someone the authorities believed to a rebel leader. There was also the need to make an example of those captured. A few days after Dixon's execution Lord Castlereagh was writing from Dublin to the Duke of Portland, the Home Secretary in London.

LETTER FROM CASTLEREAGH TO PORTLAND   *HO/100/86/P414*

22 MAY 1799

A rebel leader by the name of Dixon, but known by the title of the Northern Holt has been taken and executed. General Nugent writes [from Belfast] that by his arrest and the example made of several others, the County of Antrim is nearly in a peaceable a state as the other parts of his district. The authority of the Military Tribunals under the late Act, no longer impeded by the Clerking Jurisdiction of the Civil Courts and aided by Captain Schouler's visits to New Geneva, will, I have no doubt, keep the Country in a tolerable state of tranquillity. Summary punishment alone deters them, which it was difficult if not impossible to apply except where open rebellion prevailed before the Bill passed'.

Both Dixon and David Woods, who was also executed at the end of April, were up against rather more credible witnesses than Mayse and there seems little doubt that they were guilty of the crimes they were charged with. From Castlereagh's letter, a leader, such as Dixon, could not have expected much mercy from a court martial, although Woods refused the chance to save himself if he would give information. Both men had attempted to prosecute their rebellion with some degree of humanity and had avoided killing their opponents, even when the opportunity presented itself. Woods had robbed yeomen but not harmed them, while Dixon was able to call a yeoman in his defence, who swore that Dixon had saved his life during the attack on Randalstown the previous June. If Dixon was the flogger at M'Dowal's house, he avoided the cruder barbarities inflicted by others of his ilk, both in the United Irishmen and the military, which left their victims dead or dying. Today in County Antrim, George Dixon is ignored by history although, in another part of Ireland, one may assume that his memory would be honoured.[18]

CHAPTER 8 FOOTNOTES

1 Surprisingly there is no indication if the death sentence on John Orr of the Folly was ever carried out. A brief report in the *Belfast Newsletter* of 23 Nov 1798 stated that the sentence had been sent to Dublin for approval. He was still alive in March of 1799 when he signed a deed transferring the farm at Hurtletoot to the ownership of his son Samuel. The deed was signed in Belfast, and it may be significant that one of the witness signatures was an inn-keeper, given that the Donegal Arms in the town had been pressed into service as a temporary jail. (Reg. of Deeds 517/245/339661).

2 *Diary of an Irish Rebel.* (SRNSW ref: SZ 851; Reel 2504)

3 Statement of Samuel Humes gives details of rebel activity in Ballymena at the beginning of 1799 (Reb. Papers 620/49/19).

4 Robert Henry's statement, Reb. Papers 620/47/100.

5 Anon (1998). *The 1798 rebellion as recorded in the diaries of Gracehill Moravian Church.* p16. Reward for information on the houghing of John Stewart and statements of loyalty from the Catholic parishes of Layd, Ardclinis, Ramoan, Armoy, and Ballintoy. *BNL* 1 Jan 1799.

6 Anon (1998). *The 1798 rebellion as recorded in the diaries of Gracehill Moravian Church.* p17. Hudson 10 May 1799, Reb. Papers 620/47/16.

7 Clough incident *BNL* 23 Apr 1799; Henry O'Hara flogging *BNL* 19 April 1799; Crebilly flogging *BNL* 22 March 1799. Flogging of Swann and subsequent trial of Egelson and McDonnell *BNL* 16 & 19 April, 14 May, 7 & 18 June 1799. Swann's fate is mentioned in Smith (1996) *Memories of '98.* p23. In this account it is claimed that Swann had given information against Jack Fullarton of Limnaharry, near Kells.

8 Trial of George Dixon *BNL* 17 May 1799

9 Magill's memories in Young, *Ulster in '98. Episodes and anecdotes.*

10 Accounts of attack on the Tays see Reb. Papers 620/49/2 and trial of Dixon *BNL* 17 May 1799. for Gracehill arms see: Anon (1998). *The 1798 rebellion as recorded in the*

diaries of Gracehill Moravian Church. p17 (for 11 Jan 1799) & *BNL* 15 Jan 1799.

11 Robbery at Crebilly house *BNL* 2, 12 &19 Feb 1799. Death of William McLeverty *BNL* 17 Feb 1799.

12 Reference to Agnew's role in assisting escapes in Dickson (1960) *Revolt in the North.* Robbery at Kilwaughter in *BNL* 26 Feb, 1 & 19 March 1799. Notices concerning Agnew's resignation from the Yeomanry *BNL* 21 & 28 May 1799

13 Raids on constables: Ahoghill & Killymurris *BNL* 26 Feb 1799, Broughshane *BNL* 8 March 1799.

14 Robbery of yeomen's arms *BNL* 1 March 1799. Burning of homes in Glenarm *BNL* 15 Mar 1799. Attack on Milltown and death of Hollis *BNL* 5, 8 & 22 Feb 1799. Smith, (1996) *Memories of '98*, p 15 mentions the incident at the Milltown. In this account, written some 100 years after the event, Hollis the man killed, although a local man, was named as an attacker.

15 Leonard McNally, Reb. Papers 620/47/10; Ellis letters Reb. Papers 620/47/16 & 18; Cupples letter HO/100/86 p247. French aid was not entirely fanciful but one suspects that the French deliberately formanted belief of an imminent invasion of Ireland to distract the British Government. A French invasion fleet did set sail in late April or early May 1799, not for Ireland but to rescue the French army stranded in Egypt as a result of Napoleon's ill-fated adventure there (see HO/100/86/p369). Fortifying Antrim Market House *BNL* 26 Feb 1799; Letter from Ballymena *BNL* 15 March 1799.

16 Nugent's letter to Dublin 8 Feb 1799 (HO/100/86/p94). Martial Law Proclamation in County Antrim *BNL* 15 Mar 1799. For impact on Gracehill, see Anon (1998) *The 1798 rebellion as recorded in the diaries of Gracehill Moravian Church*, p17&18.

17 William Orr's trial *BNL* 27 May 1799. *Diary of an Irish Rebel* gives the following account of the arrest of William Orr and the interrogation of his neighbours. 'April 16 1799. I am arrested on an information of James Mayse. At 12 at night McCartney and his son John with the Antrim Yeomanry, assisted by Lieut. Murphy and the 22nd Lt Dragoons, come to the house, took me out of bed and conveyed me to Antrim Guardhouse. Same night the following persons, neighbours were arrested: Edwd McGrogan, Wm. Agnew, Frans Agnew, Saml Agnew, Saml Agnew [sic], Adw Atcheson gave himself up afterwards, Jno Kennedy and one or two more. 20th. We are all conveyed to Belfast, confined in the Provost Prison, the above persons are taken severally before a court of inquiry composed of Majors Siddon, Fox and McCoy, and in their presence the informer swears that they all assisted me in a conspiracy to take arms, after which the court explains the danger they are in and magnifys it not a little by threats of hanging each of them if they did not swear some ——— against me, that would be sufficient to do my business. This inquisition is practised for the space of 10 days, trying each of them every day, when they found threats of flogging would not make them perjurers they offered them rewards.

Note. It is remarkable that I was the only one wanted of the party, and it may be seen by their taking up so many the court had hopes of them discovering against me. Atchison was offered a reward of 500 guineas, besides his liberty and other valuable emoluments, if he'd inform against me anything that would be sufficient.'

18 Trial & execution of George Woods *BNL* 23 & 26 Apr 1799. Offer to remit his sentence if he informed is mentioned in letter from Macartney to Dublin Castle 3 May 1799 (HO/100/86/p355-7).

9
A Vision

The statement William Orr gave at his trial can be found in a collection of documents in the Public Record Office of Northern Ireland concerning the Orrs of Creavery. The series includes a small note in the handwriting of William Orr, barely three inches wide by seven inches long. One side reads as follows:

PRONI T/1956/2

A VISION

1799	Apr 16	Grew sick
	May 10	Died & sailed for unknown regions
1800	Feb 16	Crossed Styx and arrived at purgatory
1804	May 24	Embarked for the regions of bliss
	June 10	Being partly ascended by want of faith file into the infernal regions to which I descended on the 27th
	July 24	Embarked again for bliss but by mistake of the guide wanderthrough hell
	Nov 6	Embarked again for happiness and arrived at the land of ease on the 16th of Feby 1805 – Wrote the earth on the 24th May D^o 1 Feb 1806 D^o 6 Sept 1st of Nov.

The cryptic comments accompanying each date can be related to events in the life of William Orr. They encompass, what were described on his tombstone as 'the vicissitudes of his early life'. For example the date of 16 April 1799, denoted as 'Grew sick' was the date of his arrest in Antrim. The entry for 10 May 1799, 'Died and sailed for unknown regions' relates to the sentence he received at his court martial for it is the day following the start of the trial. Subsequent chapters will trace the remaining vicissitudes experienced by William Orr.

10
From New Geneva to Purgatory

William Orr may have departed as early as 11 May 1799 for the prison ship, the *William and James*, sailed from Belfast on that date. Her destination was not Prussia but rather to the south-east corner of Ireland and the estuary of the three sisters, the Rivers Barrow, Nore and Suir. Here at New Geneva, so called by Huguenots who had lived there, a temporary prison for United Irishmen had been established in the army barracks there and in prison hulks moored in the river. New Geneva was not designed as a permanent prison but rather as a clearing-house for prisoners. Sentences handed down to United Irishmen reflected a determination to get them out of Ireland and many were sentenced in 1798 to serve in the British Army. These men often ended up in regiments in the West Indies, where their chances of survival were low given the ravages of yellow fever, malaria and other tropical diseases. Others were conscripted into regiments to fight in Europe which was perhaps less hazardous and many of these men found themselves free when the Peace of Amiens was signed with France in 1803.[1]

One wonders if those who ended up in the army in Europe were considered the more willing conscripts. James Burns had operated the United Irishmen's cannon during the Battle of Antrim and found himself fighting in Europe. An associate of David Woods, Burns was from Templepatrick and was arrested early in 1799 for his persistence in the United Irish cause. He did not have the benefit of a trial before he was sent to New Geneva. Some sixty years later and a 90 year-old resident of Larne Workhouse, Burns recalled how he would have looked on the United Irishmen with less favour if he had known of the initiation oaths sworn by his comrades in the south of Ireland where recruitment was overwhelmingly Catholic. The oaths he referred to were of a sectarian nature with an obligation to do something unpleasant to Protestant heretics. Irrespective of whether or not such oaths were mere fabrications designed to discredit the Society of United Irishmen, one can easily imagine an army recruiting sergeant presenting them to the young Presbyterian from Templepatrick to persuade him to change his allegiance.[2]

By the spring of 1799, the sentence of 'serving the King of Prussia' was a common one at the Belfast court martials. It had an attraction as a propaganda weapon, for the Government used it to stir up what, now appear to be, rather persistent stereotypes of German military service. After prisoners were shipped to Germany, a Dublin report noted with glee that they would be kept tranquil there, with abstinence from whiskey and 'smart flagellation' if necessary. Those who did not behave would 'be sent to work in the mines from whence they never can return'. In reality it proved difficult to hold the Prussian king to his promise to take prisoners and comparatively few became forced recruits to his colours, probably no more than 500. Captain Schouler, mentioned in Chapter 8, had been sent to select suitable prisoners but, on his first visit to Ireland, he had decided that rebellious Irishmen might be more bother than they were worth. Agreement was only reached in May 1799 that he would take some prisoners and, even then, suitable recruits were hard to come by with Castlereagh complaining how he wished Schouler would relax his minimum height requirement. James McCambridge, one of the Antrim prisoners sent to New Geneva in 1799, was shipped to Germany. He was only 18 years of age and had not been being tried but, after he was shipped to Prussia in September 1799, it was decided that he was innocent, as the evidence against him was motivated by 'private pique and malice'. Whether he was ever extricated from Prussian service is not known.[3]

Why William Orr did not end up in Prussia is also not known but it may be that the watchmaker, if he was short like his brother John, simply did not match up to the required physical standard. Botany Bay in the recently established colony of New South Wales was to be William's destination. Although sentences of transportation were common in 1798 and 1799, Australia was an uncommon destination for these prisoners. Comparing names of those so sentenced, with those who sent there, it is apparent that only a small percentage of prisoners embarked for Australia. After the Rebellion, the first convicts did not leave for Australia until 1799 when the *Minerva* and the *Friendship* were chartered as convict ships. Together these two ships transported some 250 prisoners who can be divided into four categories.[4]

Firstly many of the prisoners transported had previously been rejected by the army as either too old, unfit or infirm. One such was James 'Jig' Fullerton, a baker from Donaghadee who had been sentenced at Newtownards to military service. In New Geneva he was judged 'unfit for any military service by the opinion and decision of the doctors'. Petitions in support of his release were sent supported by the principal inhabitants and church elders in Donaghadee. One sent by Fullerton's wife is reproduced below. These pleas for clemency met with only partial success as his sentence was commuted to seven years transportation (military service was nominally for life). A second group consisted of prisoners who, although fit for military service, were sufficiently disaffected as to deter even the British Army, a judgement which was to be confirmed by their behaviour in Australia. Other prisoners were simply 'the robbing criminality', but they were only a small proportion of those transported in 1799.[5]

TO THE MOST NOBLE MARQUIS CORNWALLIS   *SPP 595*

The Humble Petition of Elizabeth Fullerton of Donaghadee, wife to James Fullerton prisoner on board the *Friendship* transport lying at Passage near Waterford most humbly shewth – That the aforesaid prisoner was tried before Col. Atherton at Newtownards and sentenced transportation for being found in arms in the time of the rebellion – where it fully appeared that said prisoner had no command amongst the Rebels neither was he at any engagement against the Kings Army.

Bail was taken of said prisoner by Col. Ward of Bangor and sent to Genrl. Johnston at New Geneva and was never heard of since by your petitioner. Afterwards bail was taken of this prisoner by Revd. Francis Hutchenson of Donaghadee which bail and a character signed by the principal inhabitants of the place said prisoner belongs to, which My

Lord Castlereagh has been furnished with & was never heard of since by your petitioner. The sd. prisoner is lame and when inspected was returned unfit for service.

Your petitioner most humbly implores your Excellency humane consideration so far as to liberate your petitioners husband to help to maintain helpless family from whom he has been imprisoned these twelve months,

And your petitioner will forever pray etc.

ELIZA FULLERTON JUNE THE 29TH 1799.

The final category of prisoner consisted of men who had held positions of authority in the Insurgent Army or Society of United Irishmen. It may have been that William Orr fell into this group. Some of these men came from the professions and one such was Matthew Sutton who belonged to a prominent Catholic family in Wexford. Sutton had trained as a barrister and had been an officer under Father Philip Roche in the rebel army of Wexford. In the autumn of 1798, he was sentenced to transportation along with his brother, Patrick. His family was not without connections, including Archbishop Troy, the Catholic Bishop of Dublin, and strenuous attempts were made to get the two released. Patrick was freed in the autumn of 1798 but Lord Cornwallis was unwilling to release Matthew who then entertained hopes of being drafted into the army and, somewhat optimistically, even had a particular regiment in mind. In May 1799, his hopes were dashed when he was brought onboard the *Friendship* which had recently arrived at New Geneva from London. From the ship he penned a desperate letter to his father, which was forwarded to Archbishop Troy to intercede on Sutton's behalf with the authorities in Dublin Castle. The letter, reprinted here, describes conditions on board the *Friendship* and the preparations the prisoners were subjected to before their voyage. Sutton no doubt used his professional training to dramatise the situation he found himself in, but the letter does convey the terror with which he viewed a journey to the furthest ends of the earth and an unknown, wild and savage country.[6]

EXTRACTS OF LETTER FROM MATTHEW SUTTON   *SPP 846*

25 MAY 1799

I presume you have ere now heard of my being taken out of the *John & Esther* & put on board the *Friendship* of London Cpt. Reed, a convict ship bound for Botany Bay. It seems that my being attached to the 41st

[Regiment] was a mere delusion, as I understand they had no idea of placing me in that or any other regiment. Good God! What have I suffered since last Tuesday fortnight!! On that day, about four hours after I had written our worthy and invaluable friend Miss ____ from the *John & Esther*, I was brought to this vessel – my hair again cut, my cloths strip'd, placed in a tub & a Black, for Moors are the guards over us, employed in pouring bucketts of water on me till I was almost breathless. In this situation I was brought out, a shirt as coarse almost as canvass put on me, & when dressed put in irons, bolted to another unhappy man & thus guarded down to the press-room or prison, where there upwards of 120 all bolted in pairs. During the first three days of our imprisonment we had no sustenance but a little bread & water once in 24 hours. We have had since but one meal a day, consisting of about half a pound of pork or beef, & two bad biscuits; which wretched fare is handed to us between three & four o'clock, without knives, forks, plates or trenchers. A fine healthy young man has already sunk under his sufferings: he died last Sunday after an illness of three or four days. Numbers are down and to fill up the measure of our calamity, a malignant fever or epidemical disease rages in the vessel. One of the Moors died last Sunday night & another the day following. I feel my inability to convey to you in terms sufficiently descriptive the misery that surrounds & overwhelms me. The gloomy horrors that overspreads our darksound prison, the rattling of chains, the piercing cries of the sick, the heart rending sighs of those who are forever torn from their families & friends. In short the total privation of all comfort exhibit such a scene of complicated woe as should soften an adamantine breast. Two or three days after my being brought here I wrote our good friend Mr K__dy to inform my uncle, & not having heard from any friend since I fear Mr K__dy has not received my letter, & that another since to him has miscarried. I make no doubt if my situation has been known but it excited compassion & I tho' I am convinced my friends want no stimulus to their exertions, yet I think it necessary to observe that if I am not very shortly removed from this ship, I will want nothing but prayers for my soul. If it should be my misfortune to be destined for Botany Bay, I am devoted to certain death for 'tis impossible, without a miracle, that I can exist a month on the passage. I therefore entreat that immediate application may be made for me to have permission to go to America, Hamburgh, Lisbon or any other neutral place. This indulgence has been extended to many, with whom I perceive I have equal pretensions for clemency.

This letter did not win Sutton his freedom and, when the *Friendship* left New Geneva on the 15 July 1799, on board were Matt Sutton, James Fullerton and William Orr. The ship sailed along the coast to Cork to join a convoy which was assembling there. In Cork, to combat the fever epidemic on the *Friendship,* the prisoners were taken off and the ship fumigated and white-washed. On the 24 August the signal to sail was given and the *Friendship* and *Minerva* slipped out of Cork harbour along with a large fleet which was bound for America and the West Indies. After four days the two ships, with an escort vessel, left the fleet and sailed south. Each ship had on board around 130 convicts, although the precise number on the *Friendship* is uncertain as the muster roll for the ship has been lost. Almost all on the *Friendship* had been sentenced to transportation for life; an indication that they were predominantly political prisoners, as ordinary convicts usually received seven-year sentences. There were few northerners on board – apart from Orr and Fullerton, only four others can be positively identified as coming from Antrim and Down. Of these, David Bell and Hugh Devlin were among eleven prisoners who had been sentenced to serve the King of Prussia and were shipped out of Belfast on the 16 April 1799. The other two were William Briggs, later described as a gardener, and James McDonnel both of Antrim.

A Catholic Priest, James Dixon of Wexford, was on board, for it seems no other reason than he was a cousin of the notorious Thomas Dixon. Thomas, with his wife Margaret 'Mad Madge' or 'Yalla Madge', have been held responsible for the massacres which took place on the Bridge of Wexford as the Crown forces advanced on the town in 1798. Daniel McCallum was a respected physician from Dublin and he soon became the *de facto* ship's surgeon when it was discovered that the official surgeon was barely literate and had no medical training other than a few weeks served as a ship surgeon's servant. James Meehan from Offaly had been a country schoolmaster and land surveyor, a classic occupational combination in rural Ireland. Perhaps the most exalted prisoner in terms of social rank was John Brenan a former High Sheriff of Wexford. No women convicts were on board, although it seems likely that Brenan paid for his wife and children to accompany him.[7]

The initial weeks of the journey must have been a nightmare for the prisoners. Over a hundred of them, many debilitated from fever and suffering sea-sickness, were chained together in the dimly-lit hold of the ship. Slop buckets provided the toilet facilities as the 400-ton vessel sailed slowly through the nausea inducing Atlantic swell. Not all prisoners suffered to the same degree and about a dozen prisoners had been permitted to bring a supply of wine on board. This was issued sparingly by Captain Reed, who insisted that an empty bottle would be returned before he would issue a fresh bottle. The *Minerva* and *Friendship* were provided with an escort vessel for their protection but, after three week's sailing, this ship returned home. The *Minerva* was the faster of the two ships and, at the beginning of October, she sailed on ahead. Her voyage was eventful, for she was attacked by Portuguese ships and her captain made an unsuccessful attempt to capture a Spanish ship. In this later venture, Captain Cox engaged the help of Joseph Holt as a gunnery officer. Holt had become famous during the summer of 1798 for his guerrilla campaign against the army in the Wicklow Mountains but had then negotiated his own surrender in return for agreeing to transport himself and family to Australia.

The *Friendship* had no such excitements, although on occasions her crew went to battle stations when unidentified ships were sighted, but these all proved to be friendly vessels. There were no soldiers on board, either to defend the ship or to control the prisoners, for Captain Reed had found on a previous voyage that soldiers, who were often criminals drafted into the army, were themselves difficult to control. Instead he endeavoured to introduce a liberal regime on the *Friendship*, or at least liberal by the standards which then prevailed on convict ships. To avoid disputes over short rations, prisoners were deputed to weigh out their daily food allowance. Exercise on deck was permitted during the day. Some prisoners were released from their fetters soon after the ship left Cork, but it was only as the *Friendship* was crossing the Indian Ocean that this became commonplace.

However, there were vicissitudes to endure. As the ship approached the equator, she became becalmed in the Doldrums. To relieve the stifling heat beneath decks, the prisoners were dowsed with sea-water. Here, with little wind, the fever returned, killing three prisoners. Before this, the *Friendship* had called at Madeira for fresh supplies, but the symptoms of scurvy appeared among the prisoners by the time the ship reached her next port of call, St. Helena at the end of October. Here three bullocks and fresh vegetables were taken on board for the prisoners. By early December, the ship reached the Cape of Good Hope, where she stayed for two weeks but, as at previous ports, the prisoners were not permitted to leave the ship. On Christmas Eve 1799, the *Friendship* left the Cape on the last leg of the journey. The ship made good time, driven across the southern Indian Ocean by gales which led to more sea-sickness and prevented the cooking of food.[8]

All told it is believed that 19 men died on board the *Friendship* compared to only three deaths among the 131 convicts on the *Minerva*. Captain Reed recorded that he never had to punish any prisoner while his wife wrote an account of the *Friendship's* voyage which also emphasises the good behaviour of the United Irishmen. Their accounts suggest that the high mortality did not result from an especially inhuman regime on board the *Friendship* and it is more than likely that the deaths reflect the fever on the ship before she set sail. One oral history tradition from Wexford combines the fever on board the *Friendship* with Sutton's account that dark-skinned North African Moors acted as guards, for it relates that Fr. James Dixon was 'chained to a blackman until the rats ate the flesh and the corps away'.[9]

After a journey of 166 days the *Friendship* dropped anchor at Sydney on 16 February 1800. Mrs Reed recorded that the prisoners cheered as they left the ship, much to the amazement of convicts looking on from the shore who had endured harsher conditions during their transportation. William Orr, the young Calvinist from Antrim, had travelled from New Geneva to arrive in Australia, or as he put it in *A Vision* – 'Crossed Styx and arrived at purgatory'.[10]

CHAPTER 10 FOOTNOTES

1 Departure of William & James is mentioned in PRONI D/272/p47. Pakenham (1969) *Year of Liberty* (p349). Also letter (14 Nov 1799) from Mr King in London to General Littlehales in Dublin calling for a halt to sending prisoners as soldiers to the West Indies ' [soldiers there are] blacks and the whites comprised of persons and the worst of his majesty's subjects! I humbly conceive that it is the time to put and end to that mode of disembarrassing of the Irish rebels' (HO/87/p260).

2 The reminiscences of Burns, as recorded by Classon Porter, are in Young (1893). *Ulster in '98. Episodes and anecdotes.*

3 Letter from Castlereagh (18 Mar 1799) noting Schouler's arrival to select prisoners (HO/100/86/p200) and (13 May 1799) expressing relief that the King of Prussia had finally agreed to take prisoners and the return of Schouler to Ireland. 'Captain Schouler on his return to New Geneva will find a numerous and valuable aportment collected from all parts of Ireland - I wish he was not quite so scrupulous as to height – Recruits to set sail and embark at Waterford for Embden – Vessel for carrying 300 required' (HO/100/86/p375). Reference to James McCambridge as a flogger in 1799 (Reb. Papers 620/47/68). Request to return him to Ireland from Prussia (HO/100/87/p262-4)

4 For an analysis of the origins of Irish prisoners sent to New South Wales between 1799 and 1802 see Whitaker (1994) *Unfinished revolution.* p23-41. Power (1997) *The courts martial of 1798-99* gives the names of many sentenced, while Whitaker (1994) gives the names of those transported to Australia. Comparing the two, it is apparent that only a small percentage (<5%) of those sentenced to transportation were actually sent to Australia.

5 For James 'Jig' Fullerton of Donaghadee see: Trial and sentence in; Robinson (1998) *North Down and Ards in 1798* p95. Petitions for release in SPP 595. Sentence commuted to 7 years transportation in HO/100/86/p122.

6 Matthew Sutton's appeal rejected and Patrick's allowed in letter from Cornwallis 30 Oct 1798 (HO/100/86/p82).

7 Prisoner details are taken from Whitaker (1994). For details of the Dixon family of Castlebridge, Wexford see Kavanagh (1998) & Williams (1998).

8 The voyage of the *Friendship* and *Minerva* see Whitaker (1994) pp43-45. The wife of the Captain of the *Friendship*, Mary Anne Reed also wrote an anonymous account of the voyage. She describes Bryce, the ship's surgeon as 'most ignorant in his profession, otherwise illiterate yet specious and crafty. He had imposed upon the captain by a fair face and pretensions.' Later it was found that Bryce had previously been only a 'surgeon's servant'. The only punishment she recorded on the voyage was to a Chinese cook who was found to be killing the chickens kept on board for eggs in order to make broth. In: Anon (1819-20) *Cursory remarks on board the Friendship.*

9 Whitaker (1994) pp45-46. For reference to Fr. Dixon chained to a blackman; Williams (1998) p36. Mary Anne Reed's account does not mention North African Moors on board but records that the crew were mostly Lascars, Indian seamen, who did not speak English.

10 Arrival of *Friendship* in Botany Bay: Whitaker (1994) p46 & *Cursory remarks.*

11
An afflicted mother

William Orr's removal from Belfast must have caused consternation not only to his mother in Creavery, but also to her neighbours, for Edward Magrogan, Samuel Agnew and David McDowell were also sent to New Geneva. Other arrests were to follow. In June 1799 Daniel Taggart of Dunsilly was accused of being with 'an armed banditti' concerned in 'breaking open and feloniously entering divers houses and plundering them of arms'. Three miles away in Browndodd, Walter McCreary was thrown into prison accused as being 'a person of infamous and wicked character' who 'did aid and abet and assist in flogging George Robinson of the Braid, a constable'. Whether as a response to the arrests or not, the security situation in Antrim had improved dramatically by June 1799, to the extent that Castlereagh could report on the changed outlook of Presbyterians in County Antrim who were increasingly joining the establishment forces of the yeomanry and the Orange Order.[1]

Magrogan, Agnew and McDowell were to spend 20 months in New Geneva without the benefit of a trial. Their freedom was not obtained lightly, as each prisoner had to produce two men who would each stand bail for his good behaviour for what was then the considerable sum of £200. In turn, these bail bonds had to be approved by magistrates who also had to support the petition requesting the prisoner's release. Petitions for the release of Agnew, Agnew and McDowell survive. David McDowall was described in his petition of November 1800 as a weaver. The petition had the backing of Jackson Clarke and Samuel Allen, the magistrate who had committed him 'by order of Lieut. Col. Leslie on the evidence of James Maize'. The local Church of Ireland vicar of Donegore & Kilbride also wrote 'I do hereby certify that I do personally know the within named David McDowall, he being born in this parish of quiet honest dissenting Protestant parents & is himself a quiet honest, sober & industrious young man as I never knew or heard anything prejudiced to his character but the information he was taken up for, which I believe was perfectly false'. Samuel Agnew, who was a farmer & shop keeper from Donegore, and James Beck of Rathmore Trench (beside Farranshane), a cloth merchant, each agreed to stand surety for the sum of £200.[2]

The petitions for Magrogan and Agnew, reproduced below, indicate the efforts made to refute the evidence of James Maize, who had identified them as accomplices of William Orr. Samuel Agnew of Dunsilly had arranged that James Lawther of Dunsilly, farmer, and Samuel Redmond of Thornhill would each stand surety for £200 for seven years. Again it was Jackson Clarke who vouched for his release along with Rev. Macartney, but Major James Drummond, who commanded the Northern Army District from Belfast, was non-committal on Agnew's innocence, merely commenting that: 'Sir, I have the honour to enclose a petition from Samuel Agnew with a recognizance. The man was taken up nearly two years ago and has been in confinement ever since in New Geneva - Several others of the same party in which he was apprehended have been liberated.' Vicar Macartney was not so reticent and added an exasperated footnote: 'I certify, <u>as I have frequently done to Government before</u>, that Samuel Agnew surrendered himself to me & that I [am] convinced from a variety of circumstances that the magistrates who examined into his case in Belfast were imposed upon & that I am convinced in my own mind that he was innocent of any charge laid before him.'

PETITION OF EDWARD MAGROGAN TO   *SPP 701*
HAVE HIS SON EDWARD RELEASED

To Lord Castlereagh. That a malignant fellow [Maize] whose fortune was deplorable, made information against petitioners son Edward Magrogan

that he was concerned in the late rebellion in consequence the Rev. Dr
Macartney of Antrim, Captain Constantine and Lieutenant Murphy
repaired to petitioner's dwelling from which said son was then absent,
but petitioner being thoroughly convinced he was culpable went for and
delivered him to said gentleman, who committed him to Belfast, from
which he was transported to New Geneva, where he remains. Gentlemen
considering him innocent and feeling for him and petitioner £200 bail
was given Dr Macartney (a magistrate) for said son's good behaviour etc.
Since which petitioner applied to General Drummond at Belfast for his
liberation, who kindly advised petitioner to apply to your Lordship.
Petitioner saith that the lad was industrious of good principles and
demeanour, and the chief assistant petitioner had to support a poor
family who now experiences the effects of his absence. Therefore
petitioner humbly begs your Lordship out of your humanity and
goodness to the distressed may commiserate his situation and order said
son enlargement and for Your Lordship's prosperity etc petitioner will
fervently pray.

Petitioner further saith that Thomas Agnew was in Scotland at the time
of arms was lifted by the insurgents in this country, which can be proved
by several oaths, notwithstanding the informer had him first upon his list
in company with William Orr, and the above Edward can declare on oath
he never saw David McDowel until saw him prisoner in Belfast tho' said
informer mentioned them to be all of the said company lifting arms
together.

  EDWARD McGROGAN   ANTRIM SEPT. 25 1799

PETITION FOR SAMUEL AGNEW   *SPP 628*

To his excellency Marquis Cornwallis, Dublin Castle, Lieutenant
General, General Governor of his majesties Kingdom of Ireland. The
memorial of Samuel Agnew late of Dunsilly in the County of Antrim but
now a prisoner in New Geneva Barracks. Most Humbly shewth; That
memorialist had the misfortune to be implicated with being concerned in
the late unhappy troubles in this country & being willing to submit to the
laws on hearing that he was so charged memorialist came and surrendered
himself to the Revd Geo. Macartney who sent memorialist to Belfast
where he remained until he was sent to New Geneva where he now
remains without being charged or even knowing what it is he charged
with. That memorialist from his long confinement is very much impaired
in his health and finding that many persons in a similar situation has been
liberated thro' your Excellency's goodness and humanity on bail. Meml.

has procured bail to be given before two magistrates of the Co. of Antrim for his allegiance and good behaviour which he has taken the liberty to enclose & therefore Meml humbly implores your Excellency in your well known human goodness & humanity to order Meml to be liberated on enclosed recognizances as in duty bound will ever pray.

SAML. AGNEW   8TH DEC. 1800.

Born in 1740, the son of a High Sheriff of County Antrim, George Macartney BA, MA, LLB, LLD remains one of the more colourful characters to have occupied the pulpit of All Saints Church of Ireland in Antrim. He has left no great legacy as a preacher or evangelist but rather, operating in an age when to be a vicar of the Church of Ireland was to be in possession of 'a living', Macartney's reputation is for his avarice in the collection of parishes. Two days after the death of Rev. William McCleverty was announced in February 1799, the *Newsletter* reported Macartney had been granted by the Marquis of Donegal, to whom he was 'first chaplain', McCleverty's parishes of Skerry, Racavan and Glynn. Macartney could add these to his existing parishes of Templepatrick, Duneane, Cranfield and Antrim where he had been rector and magistrate since 1773. Together they contained a numerous flock who provided a rich income of church tithes, but very few belonged to the Church of Ireland and, for those who did, Macartney would install a poorly paid curate.[3]

Before and after the Rebellion, Macartney had been active in arresting those suspected of sedition but he behaved erratically during the Battle of Antrim. At a point when it seemed that Antrim had fallen to the rebels, Macartney and John Staples abandoned not only the town, but Macartney's two sons who were in the yeomanry there, to sail across Lough Neagh. Macartney claimed this was to raise the alarm in County Tyrone, but the fact that the two chose the shore of the Lough furthest away from Antrim, involving a journey of five hours at least, suggests he thought the Loyalist cause had been lost in County Antrim. Later, in a letter to the Lord Lieutenant in Dublin, Lord Massereene referred to Macartney's conduct during the Battle of Antrim as 'running away from this town on the approach of the enemy and remaining away for 10 days'. Macartney had managed the 2nd Earl of Massereene's affairs in the 1780s when the Earl was incarcerated in a debtors' prison in Paris. Massereene could have easily settled with his creditors if he had had the mind to and it was only the French Revolution which led to his release. By the early 1800s, when Massereene made his comments regarding Macartney, relations between the two were poisonous which has been attributed to the malign influence of Massereene's second wife, Elizabeth Blackburn. She had formerly been his mistress and, prior to that, had been a London servant whom, it was alleged, his Lordship had become infatuated with by the dexterity with which she twirled her mop![4]

It is clear from the note accompanying Agnew's appeal that Macartney had come to believe that the evidence of James Maize was false. Macartney was of this opinion in the summer of 1799 when he supported a petition from Elizabeth Orr to halt or at least postpone William Orr's transportation. However by the time the secretary in Dublin Castle, Marsden, wrote to Cork, the *Friendship* had already left for Australia. Marsden then advised Mrs Orr not to make further advice for a period of three years – suggesting that he and the authorities in Dublin Castle were not convinced that her son was completely innocent of United Irish involvement. Mrs Orr bided her time until 1805 when she made another attempt to obtain her son's release as follows:

PP&C 1140

STATE [SIC] OF WIDOW ORR'S CASE OF THE PARISH OF ANTRIM IRELAND concerning her son William Orr, watchmaker Jan the 26 1805. In the year 1799 an Informans [sic] person thro' malice made a false information against said son that he was concerned in lifting arms, That strict enquiry being made by the Reverend Doctor Macartney of said parish, magistrate of the County of Antrim, & his reverence finding the information false and unfounded, He thro' humanity wrote with said widow to the Right Honourable Lord Castlereagh, which on perusal his Lordship ordered his secretary Mr Marsden to write to Cork where said son was on board a transport bound for Botany Bay for him to be exchanged (?) to which Mr Marsden received an answer (as he told her) that the transport had sailed a fortnight before the arrival of his letter. On her requesting the Secretaries advice for her not to make further application for the space of three years.

That said period being some years elapsed & said son still in Botany Bay, she therefore humbly requests that the case of an afflicted mother may be taken to consideration for a beloved son so that said son may have permission to return to his native country to be a comfort to her in the decline of her life & in duty bound she will sincerely pray for her benefactors prosperity etc.

28 Jan 1805

ELIZABETH ORR

Macartney again supported her plea and he wrote to Lord Castlereagh, recounting the inconsistencies in the case and his previous support for Agnew and McDowell. Indeed, against all odds and the history of the Orr and Macartney families being so diametrically opposed to each other in the years leading up to 1798, a bond of friendship had arisen between the ageing vicar and Widow Orr.

PP&C 1140

THE RIGHT HONOURABLE LORD VISCT. CASTLEREAGH, HOUSE OF COMMONS, LONDON

MY LORD   ANTRIM 29TH JANUARY 1805

In addition to what is mentioned in Widow Orr's statement respecting her son which is enclosed, I know that two men whose names are McDowall & Agnew were charged with being with William Orr in the act of taking up the Arms alluded to, for which offence they were all imprisoned & that upon strict enquiry I found it impossible that the charge could be true, they being at the hour stated in the charge stated at places 17 miles distant, and from the circumstance of the evidence, who was a deserter having declared that he would injure the parties whom he charged, and the persons from the arms were taken denying they were the persons who took the arms. Added to the circumstances of the Persons being of good character, who proved that the persons charges were at places 17 miles distant at the time the deserter swore the arms were taken up, on my representation of these facts supported by affidavits to Government, they McDowal & Agnew were released.

I should therefore suppose My Lord (from these circumstances having occurred since interference from W^{idow} Orr mentioned in the enclosed statement, which would have ended in his liberation had the order arrived previous to the sailing of the transport) that your Lordship will have the goodness in Compassion for the poor widow to procure an order to the Governor of Port Jackson to release him – the unfortunate man (who is a watchmaker) says (that the Governor from his good opinion of his conduct has made him free at the colony) in a letter to his mother date 8th August 1803 Port Jackson.

This young man Wm. Orr and Agnew who is now at liberty were both apprehended by me, and your Lordship may be assured I should not say what I have done if I did not think it safe for the country, as well as justice to Wm. Orr, that he should be permitted to return, the Persons having been set at liberty who were charged unjustly by the same evidence, the Deserter - You know *parva componere magnis* that your

Lordship & I were coadjutors in putting down the baneful Rebellion in Ireland, I therefore am convinced that you will not look upon this application as an intrusion, particularly as I have no intercourse with the Government here – May I request for the satisfaction of the poor mother, that you will forward the enclosed letter to her son by the same conveyance which carries his discharge, if he is discharged & that you will favour me with an answer, as he is anxious the answer of this application in favour of her son, I am with great respect Your Lordship's faithful & obedient Servant

GEO. MACARTNEY[5]

Castlereagh's memory of the first petition on Orr's behalf in 1799 was rather hazy but he nevertheless replied to Macartney in favourable terms:

PRONI T/1956/4

TO THE REV. GEO. MACARTNEY ANTRIM

I have received your letter of the 29th of last month respecting William Orr and in enclosing a paper containing his mother's statement of his case. I cannot at present call to my recollection the circumstance mentioned in that paper of my having interfered in Orr's favour - but I shall not fail to take an early opportunity of communicating your letter and enclosure to Mr Marsden in order that every justice may be done to W. Orr which his case may appear to merit.

I am, dear sir, your faithful & obedient honourable servant

CASTLEREAGH

By March Whitehall bureaucracy had swung into action as the following letter shows:

PRONI T/1956/5

LETTER TO ALEXANDER MARSDEN ESQ. WHITEHALL   18 MARCH 1805

Sir

I have laid before Lord Hawkesbury [the Home Secretary] your letter of the 13th of this month signifying The Lord Lieutenant's request that William Orr, a convict who was transported to New South Wales in the year 1799 may be permitted to return to Ireland by the first opportunity, as there is reason to believe that Orr was unjustly charged with the offence for which he was transported.

In reply I am directed to acquaint you for the information of the Lord Lieutenant that no time has been lost in making a communication upon the subject to the Colonial Department, with a view to His Excellency's desire being complied with.

I am etc.

J. KING

The same day, King sent a note to Edward Cooke who was under-secretary to the colonies.

CO 201

JOHN KING TO EDWARD COOKE   18 MARCH 1805

Within, I transmit to you by the direction of Lord Hawkesbury, the copy of a letter which I have received from Mr Marsden signifying the request of His Excellency the Lord Lieutenant [of Ireland] that, for the reasons therein mentioned, William Orr, a convict, who was transported in 1799, may be permitted to return to Ireland, and I am to desire that you will lay same before Lord Camden and, move his Lordship to be pleased to give directions to the Governor of New South Wales, for complying with His Excellency's desire.

This decision to allow William Orr to return was not conveyed directly to Mrs Orr in Creavery but to Macartney in Antrim.

PRONI T/1956/6

LETTER TO REVD DOCTOR MACARTNEY, ANTRIM   DUBLIN CASTLE
23 MARCH 1805

Sir

In consequence of a representation laid before the Lord Lieutenant of the case of William Orr of the Parish of Antrim who was transported to New South Wales in the year 1799, His Excellency has recommended that he should be permitted to return to Ireland, and I have the honour to send you a copy of a letter from the Under Secretary of State signifying that the necessary steps will be immediately taken agreeably to the His Excellency's desire.

I have the honour to be, Sir, Your most obedient humble servant

A MARSDEN

Widow Orr's pleas had born fruit in a relatively modest period of under two months. However it was to be almost another four months before the order to release her son was finally approved. On the 13 July 1805 Castlereagh, who was now Secretary of State for the Colonies wrote to Philip Gidley King, Governor of New South Wales:

CO 201

LORD CASTLEREAGH TO PHILIP GIDLEY KING   13 JULY 1805

I transmit to you a copy of a letter from Mr King, enclosing one from Mr Marsden, signifying the request of His Excellency the Lord Lieutenant of Ireland that, William Orr, a convict, who was transported in 1799, may be permitted to return to Ireland and as there appears reason to conclude in consequence of his good conduct you have already granted him his freedom, and I am to desire that the said William Orr may be permitted to avail himself of the first opportunity of returning to that kingdom. In the event of his not having received the pardon above averted to, You will consider yourself so authorized hereby to extend His Majesty's Gracious Mercy to him.

All that now remained was for Elizabeth Orr to wait patiently for her son to appear. A return journey to Australia journey could take a year or more so she could not expect to greet him until the autumn of 1806.

CHAPTER 11 FOOTNOTES

1 Castlereagh's letter to London 3 June 1799 (HO/100/87pp5-8). Castlereagh also commented on the strength of the linen industry in the North - 'never at any former period so prosperous.' From Portglenone, Rev. Hudson also remarked on the change in outlook in June 1799 and noted the high prices received by the weavers. The price of linen, he declared was 'the pulse of the North' (Reb. Papers 620/47/19). Also in June, the loyal subjects living in and around Randalstown were confident enough to publish a declaration of loyalty (*BNL* 4 June 1799).

2 David McDowal SPP 493 & 496; Samuel Agnew SPP 628; Edward Magrogan SPP 701.

3 Glendinning (1996) *Celebrating 400 years 1596-1996 All Saints Parish Church, Antrim.* Transfer of McLeverty's parishes *BNL* 19 Mar 1799.

4 Massereene's letter to Lord Hardwicke 28 May 1803 in: Malcomson (1972) *The extraordinary career of the 2nd Earl of Massereene, 1743-1805* pp101-103. Also p121 for Mrs Blackburn's skill with the mop: 'She possessed a peculiar dexterity of twirling her mop and his Lordship admired her dexterity so much that he fell in love with this fair twirler'.

5 Port Jackson is now better known as Sydney. *'parva componere magnis'* – short for '*si parva licet componere magnis'* (Virgil) – if it is permissible to compare small things to great. Macartney's rather haughty comment 'I have no intercourse with the Government here [i.e. in Dublin]' drew a sceptical if illegible response in a note scribbled by Marsden to King: ' March 6 1805. It seems right from the circumstances stated by Mrs Elizabeth Orr that her son William Orr should have permission to return & Dr Macartney should be informed of this at the same time – as [to] the declaration made by Dr Macartney, a magistrate, that he has no intercourse with the King's Government in Ireland & more especially as I recollect having received letters from him myself respecting the case of the unfortunate Mr O'Hara.' (PP&C 1140).

12
Embarking for the regions of bliss

The colony of New South Wales was only 12 years old when William Orr arrived there in 1800. The population was small with hardly more than 5000 Europeans located in scattered settlements along the coastline around Botany Bay and Port Jackson. About 40 per cent of these were convicts, so that the free settlers and the colonial establishment headed by the Governor, John Hunter, constituted barely a majority. The arrival of the *Minerva* and *Friendship* prison ships, with their comparatively exotic cargo of United Irishmen, unsettled Hunter, not least because of the social status of some prisoners. Writing to London in March 1800 about the new arrivals he complained:

> Many of these prisoners have either been bred up in genteel
> life, or to professions unaccustom'd to hard labor. These are a
> dead weight on the public store; and really, my Lord,
> notwithstanding we cannot fail to have the utmost abhorrence
> of the crimes which sent many of them here, yet we can
> scarcely divest ourselves of the common feelings of humanity
> so far as to send a physician, a formerly respectable sheriff of

a county, a Roman Catholic priest, or a Protestant clergyman
and family to the grubbing hoe or timber carriage. Amongst
the lower classes there are many old men unfit for anything
but what we call huttkeepers, who stay at home to prevent
robbery whilst the rest of the inhabitants of the hutt are at
labor.[1]

Fearing the new arrivals' political opinions, the Governor was soon
making arrangements to secure the gunpowder magazine in the colony
from a surprise attack. For their part, and as soon as they had found their
feet, many United Men continued on as before, forming Societies, issuing
passwords and planning for a fresh insurrection. Existing prisoners were
recruited, but this was always a hazardous process as the more astute of
these saw the opportunity of gaining favours by informing. A rebellion
was planned for September 1800 but narrowly averted through intelligence
provided by informers. Conspirators were caught, sentenced to flogging
and transported to Norfolk Island in the Pacific where, undaunted, they
began to plot another rising. In December, the Norfolk Island rising was
prevented, but only at the last moment. Two conspirators were then
executed without trial and others flogged, including some soldiers who
were implicated in the conspiracy.

By 1804, the arrival of five more convict ships from Ireland had
reinforced the United Irishmen in New South Wales. A rising took place
in March of that year when upwards of 400 men attempted to gain control
of the colony with the cry of 'Liberty or Death and a ship to take us
home'. As ever, the rebels were chronically short of fire power and were
easily suppressed after an unequal battle with the garrison of the colony,
in which about 20 rebels died. One of the leaders of the Castle Hill
Rebellion, as it has been styled, was Samuel Humes of Moneydaff, a
townland not far from Cloughmills in County Antrim. Humes had been
involved in seizing arms during 1799 and was transported after his court
martial in 1800. His voyage on the *Hercules* transport ship was marked
by a mutiny which was brutally suppressed after which no little cruelty
was inflicted on the prisoners. Humes prospered in Australia and, by the
time of the rebellion, was overseer of the Government carpenters at Castle
Hill where he had his own house. Despite his comparatively comfortable
circumstances, he cast his lot with the rebels and was executed immediately
after a court martial on 8 March 1804.[2]

The more educated convicts took care to stay aloof from attempts at insurrection and, despite Governor Hunter's initial misgivings, were soon putting their talents to good use in the colony. Many had been granted ticket-of-leave status by the summer of 1801 which enabled them to work for an employer or on their own account but their movement in the colony was restricted. In January 1802 some had obtained further emancipation with the granting of conditional pardons, which allowed them freedom to live where they wished in the colony but forbade them to return to Ireland or Britain. Matthew Sutton was among the first ticket-of-leave prisoners and he opened a school in Sydney in 1801. Unfortunately for him, this was done without the permission of the new governor, the capricious Philip King, who moved Sutton to the Paramatta settlement, where he acted as clerk to the magistrate's court. Sutton benefited from a conditional pardon in 1802, but three years later he was sent to Norfolk Island after a 10 gallon keg of spirits was found buried in his garden. Illegal distilling was a favourite occupation of many convicts and free settlers in the colony. James Fullerton was also granted ticket of leave status in 1801 and operated as a baker. James Brennan, the former Sheriff of Wexford, was soon running a 90 acre farm for a settler and then, after his conditional pardon, a 100 acre farm on his own account.

William Orr did not receive his conditional pardon until 4th June 1803, although he was listed as a watchmaker in the colony as early as 1801. He must have written of his pardon to his mother in August 1803, given Macartney's comments to Castlereagh that Governor King had made Orr 'free at the colony'. In the New South Wales Archives there is a notebook with entries which Orr made around this time, describing the events leading up to his arrest and trial which have been referred to earlier. The notebook also contains charges for watch repairs that he had carried out. Among Orr's customers were Governor King and army officers, as well as United Irishmen such as Hugh Devlin of Belfast and Dr McCallum. Also in the list was a Captain Wilson. The same page shows expenditure on a house, with debts incurred for 'making a gate, window shutters, altering doors, a beadstead and doors', suggesting that Orr was fitting out a house. Apart from this notebook, there is no indication of Orr's activities in New South Wales, other than he was a visitor to the house of Maurice Margarot. One of the so-called Scottish Martyrs, Margarot had been secretary of the London Corresponding Society which had strong republican tendencies and promoted Paine's *Rights of Man* in England. He was convicted and transported after attending the British Convention of the Friends of the People in Edinburgh in 1794 and his house in Sydney was described as 'the most seditious house in the country'.[3]

Given that he was to all intents a free man and his bills for repairing a house, it might have been thought that William Orr would have been content to bide his time in Australia. But no, when his pardon arrived in Sydney early in 1806, he was no longer in the colony. Governor King's reply to Lord Castlereagh, on the 27 July 1806, noted that: '[Orr] having received a conditional emancipation, found means to secret himself on an American vessel in 1804 when he left this colony. Since when a report has prevailed that he died upon that vessel. However in compliance with your Lordship's directions, his free pardon was inserted in the *Sydney Gazette*, 4th May 1806'.[4]

It is now impossible to know why Orr left. Was it on the spur of the moment, prompted simply an unexpected opportunity of escape or was it the subject of long months of planning? Given his expenditure on a house, the former seems more likely. A possibility is that it was prompted in some way by the Castle Hill Rebellion in March 1804, with the execution of eight men, the public flogging of others, a tightening of security and perhaps a feeling of animosity against the Irish convicts as Governor King sought out co-conspirators.

Escaping from Botany Bay was not common-place but not unknown. Although prisoners occasionally attempted to high-jack a ship, the best means of escape were to either stow-away or hitch a lift on a visiting ship. Often these were American whalers which called into Port Jackson, the type of ship referred to by Governor King. Calcutta was in many ways a tempting destination for escapees as it was the nearest large English speaking city to New South Wales. But it did not welcome either escaped or freed convicts as is shown by the experience of the *Minerva* when she arrived there in 1800. After the *Minerva* discharged her cargo of United Irishmen in Port Jackson, her master recruited recently released convicts to work their passage to Calcutta, the next port of call. These were among the first prisoners to have completed their sentences in Botany Bay but, for a released but penniless ex-prisoner, it was difficult to leave Australia once his or her sentence was completed especially as shipping was curtailed by the wars in Europe.

There was consternation in Calcutta amongst the East India Company officials when the *Minerva* docked with 24 ex-convicts and one escaped convict, Thomas Parnell, on board. Parnell had remained in the ship's hold for nine days, getting only 'so much water as he could procure by dipping the end of his handkerchief into a water cask'. In Calcutta he was arrested and returned to New South Wales. The Company was equally keen to rid itself of the others and it made sure they were enlisted on outgoing ships. A letter was sent to New South Wales stating that the Company was determined not to allow the 'worst kind of adventurers [i.e. ex convicts] taking root' and 'considering it essential to the good order of the British Territories and in other respects of considerable importance to the Company's interest that convicts from New South Wales not be permitted to establish themselves at any of the British Settlements or in any part of India'.[5]

On 24 May 1804 the *Mersey* left Sydney carrying a cargo of timber and bound for Calcutta under the command of Captain James Wilson. Governor King had chartered the ship for the return journey to bring 250 cows from Bengal to Hobart, Tasmania. Her route was northwards along the coast before turning west through the Torres Straits, which separate Australia from New Guinea. The Straits are strewn with rocky islets and submerged reefs but British ships had no reliable chart to guide them through these hazardous waters. In mid-June the *Mersey* foundered in the Torres Straits and the ship and her cargo were lost. Captain Wilson and sixteen or seventeen of his crew were able to save themselves but, as the ship is believed to have been carrying 73 people, over 50 of those on-board had drowned. With the survivors in the *Mersey's* long-boat, Wilson endeavoured to reach a safe port, not an easy task as Britain was at war with the Dutch, so rendering the Dutch East India Settlements unsafe for British shipping. Continuing to sail westwards, Wilson put into the Portuguese settlement of Dili on the island of Timor, some 1200 miles west of the Torres Straits. He only stopped there long enough to make his craft more sea worthy before setting sail again, covering a further 1500 miles to his next port of call; the British East India Company settlement of Bencoolen, now Bengakulu, on the island of West Sumatra. There, Wilson procured a passage on a local ship to Madras, from where he sailed as a passenger on the *Margaret*, arriving in Calcutta on the 9 September. By this time the surviving members of his crew had become dispersed for it was two weeks later that the *Mersey's* surgeon made it to Calcutta. Following Wilson's arrival in Calcutta, the *Calcutta Gazette* carried reports of the shipwreck of the *Mersey* and the details of Wilson's epic voyage. News of the sinking reached Sydney in November 1804, with the arrival of a ship from Dili, but it was not until the following April that news of Wilson's safe arrival in Calcutta was finally received in Sydney.[6]

Capt. Wilson's eventful voyage agrees so closely with the dates and allegories listed in William Orr's *A Vision* for 1804 that it seems certain the Orr escaped from Australia on the *Mersey* only to endure shipwreck. Indeed, the entry in Orr's account book of a watch repair for a Captain Wilson in 1804, provides a potential point of contact between the two men. Calcutta and Bengal in *A Vision*, become 'the regions of bliss' and 'the land of ease' as is confirmed by a note on the reverse of *A Vision* stating 'Arrived Calcutta 16th February 1805' which is the date given for arriving 'at the land of ease'. Comparing the chronology of *A Vision* with that of the *Mersey*'s voyage, the ship's departure date coincides with the entry 'embarked for the regions of bliss.' The next entry for June 10 'Being partly ascended by want of faith file into the infernal regions to which I descended on the 27th' therefore refers to the wreck of *Mersey* while 'the infernal regions to which I descended on the 27th [June]' would be the arrival of the *Mersey's* long-boat in Dili. As the long boat required a refit to make her more seaworthy, the next date, 24 July, and entry 'Embarked again for bliss but by mistake of the guide wander through hell' is the departure from Dili.

The meaning of 'but by mistake of the guide wander through hell' is unclear but can be understood if Wilson left some of the survivors behind in Bencoolen to make their own way to India as best they could. For Orr, an escaped convict with presumably little money, this may have been sufficiently hellish experience as to justify the description. It appears that he did not leave for India until 6 November which is accompanied by the entry 'Embarked again for happiness and arrived at the land of ease on the 16th of Feby 1805 - Wrote the earth on the 24th May, Ditto 1 Feb 1806, Ditto 6 Sept 1st of Nov.' The boat which may have taken him there was the ship *George*, which the *Calcutta Gazette* reported as arriving in the river at Calcutta on 14 February 1805, having sailed from Rangoon. The final references in *A Vision* referring to 'Wrote the earth' most likely refer to letters Orr sent back to Ireland.

William Orr's escape from Sydney to Calcutta with its shipwreck, weeks spent in an open long-boat in tropical seas, stranded if not abandoned in exotic towns can surely be numbered along with his arrest, trial and transportation as additional vicissitudes of his early life.

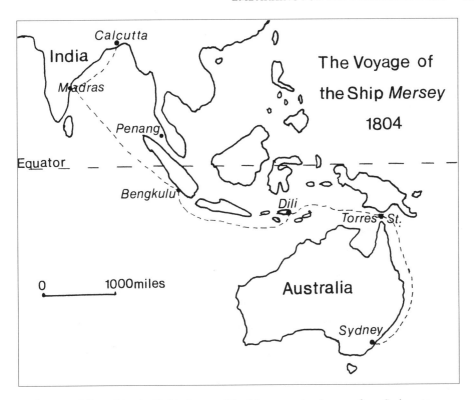

The route followed by the ill-fated crew of the Mersey on her journey from Sydney to Calcutta in 1804.

CHAPTER 12 FOOTNOTES

1 Whitaker (1994) *Unfinished revolution*. p46. Subsequent events in New South Wales described in this chapter are also taken from *Unfinished Revolution*.

2 Humes arrest and sentence (Reb. Papers 620/49/17&19).

3 *Diary of an Irish Rebel*. (SRNSW ref: SZ851; Reel (2504)).

4 Philip Gidley King to Lord Castlereagh 27 July 1806. CO 201.

5 Arrival of *Minerva* in Calcutta and response of East India Company: Bengal Dispatches 1807-1811 (IOR O/5/25).

6 Voyage of the *Mersey*: Bateson, *Australian Shipwrecks (vol. 1 1622-1850)* p40 & Nicholson, *Gazetteer of Sydney Shipping 1788-1840*. Bateson gives the wrong year (23-24 May 1805) for the departure of the *Mersey*, an error noted by Nicholson. In the *Sydney Gazette* of 24 May 1804 gives the *Mersey's* departure as on 27 May 1804, her wreck was reported on 25 Nov 1804 and Capt. Wilson's arrival in Calcutta reported on 14 April 1805. Also reports in *Calcutta Gazette* of 27 Sept & 4 Oct 1804.

13
Your friend and well-wisher

When William Orr arrived in Calcutta in 1805, it was rapidly acquiring the trappings of a great imperial city as the capital of the ever-expanding British Empire in India and the Far East. His priorities were to avoid the attention of the authorities with the risk of arrest and deportation back to Australia and to earn enough money to support himself. His cousin's execution in 1797 had achieved notoriety beyond the shores of Ireland and it can be well imagined that, even in Bengal, the name of William Orr was redolent of sedition and the United Irishmen. It is of little surprise then, that the lists of European inhabitants of Calcutta in the early 1800s do not include William Orr, watchmaker but rather William Jamieson, watchmaker. This was to be the alias which William Orr assumed for a period of 16 years.[1]

The final entries of *A Vision,* record that 'he wrote the earth', firstly in May 1805 and then on 1 Feb. 1806. The second of these letters was sent to his mother as it was referred to in the reply sent to Calcutta. This second letter may have been in response to a reply from his first letter to Antrim, although the interval of nine months between the two is barely sufficient time for this, given the long return voyage between India and England.

Writing home to Antrim was not without risk, for the postal service of the early nineteenth century was a rather more public enterprise than the anonymous service of today. William Orr could, no doubt visualise the interest which a letter from India to his mother would create when it arrived with the Antrim postmaster, for it would hardly pass unnoticed. Such a letter could easily pass into the hands of a local magistrate and so reveal Orr's alias and place of abode. To avoid this, his letter was addressed to Samuel Redmond of Thornhill, a house still standing in Lisnevenagh townland, next to Creavery. Redmond's business interests may have been judged more likely to have involved a communication from India. At any rate William Orr must have trusted the discretion of Sam Redmond who, as we have seen, had stood surety for Samuel Agnew's release in 1800.[2]

It took five months for William Orr's letter sent in February 1806 to reach Creavery. Shortly after its arrival, Mrs Orr received a visit from the Rev. George Macartney. In 1805, Macartney had moved his residence from Belmont in Antrim to White Hall near Ballymena to be closer to the Dervock estate of his kinsman, Earl Macartney of Lissanure. The Rev. Macartney was acting as agent for this estate, having abandoned Antrim to the care of a curate. In addition Macartney may have considered there was little reason for him to stay in Antrim, where the eccentric second Earl of Massereene had died in the previous year. Massereene had married Mrs Blackburn in 1802, but then had died childless. Although his title passed to his brother, he had bequeathed his considerable estates to Mrs Blackburn. She now lived in the castle with her mysterious companion, the former Catholic Priest O'Doran and his son. Macartney would testify as to the malign influence of Mrs Blackburn in the third Earl's legal challenge to his brother's will and one can imagine that Macartney would have been reluctant to meet the Dowager Lady Massereene at Sunday service in Antrim.[3]

The Thornhill Road passes through Creavery and was the main highway from Antrim to Ballymena in 1806. On 30 July 1806, when travelling to Ballymena, Macartney decided to call on Mrs Orr, perhaps to report the absence of news from Australia regarding William Orr's pardon. He arrived to a scene of activity in the Orr household as William's brother John prepared to leave for Derry. John Orr had fled to America in 1798, but it shows how relaxed the atmosphere in County Antrim had become, that he had been able to return home and was openly living with his mother. Mrs Orr may have been alarmed to see her visitor, for she knew that Macartney was no fool and would inquire as to the cause of the activity which he found in Creavery. Overcoming any misgivings, she decided to take Macartney into her confidence and showed him William's latest letter which had requested that £100 be sent to Calcutta. It was to arrange this payment through 'friends of Mr Alexander the Hindostan Banker at Calcutta' that John Orr was about to set off for Derry.

India would have been much to the fore in Macartney's thoughts at the time, for his son John was serving in the army near Lucknow. John's health had been failing and Macartney had endeavoured to get his son transferred from his cavalry regiment to the less arduous work of land surveying. In February 1806, the situation had become more serious when Macartney received the disturbing news that John's health had deteriorated and he was now trying to engineer his son's return home. Unbeknown to Macartney and at the very time he was visiting Creavery, John was enduring some very real vicissitudes of his own. For Europeans with failing health in India it was common to take to the sea for recuperation, and in March 1805 John Macartney sailed on a trading ship, the *Henry Addington*, from Calcutta which was bound for Indonesia. Pirates captured the ship on the 28 May 1805 and John Macartney with 28 others were set adrift in the ship's long-boat. They safely made their way to Sumatra where, with the aid of a friendly local prince, they were able to join an English vessel, *Warren Hastings*, and set sail again. Within days however the *Warren Hastings* was attacked and captured after a day-long chase, this time by a French frigate, the *Semillante*. The French refused to release the crew or passengers but kept them as hostages to be exchanged for French prisoners. John Macartney was to spend almost a year in captivity in Île de Bourbon, before being released in May 1806.[4]

Macartney did not disappoint Mrs Orr's confidence in him and quickly proposed a method of facilitating the transfer of £100 money to Calcutta which would circumvent the troublesome charges and sloth of early nineteenth century banking and save John Orr a journey to Derry. Macartney's proposal was simple. He had a nephew, Alexander Stewart, who was a lawyer in Calcutta. Stewart's mother lived at Ballytweedy House, about five miles from Antrim on the Seven Mile Straight. John Orr would give Mrs Stewart the £100, while Macartney would arrange that Counsellor Stewart in Calcutta would give William Orr the same amount. Mrs Orr readily agreed to this proposal, for, on the following day, 31 July 1806, Macartney penned a long letter to William Orr telling him of his plan. In the letter, partly reproduced here, Macartney goes to some length to explain his sorrow at William's arrest and the high opinion he now had of him and his immediate family. In addition Macartney copied out the letters of pardon which Orr could use to avoid arrest.

For Macartney, India was a place where a fortune could be made and his letter makes it clear that he thought Orr should stay in Calcutta so that he could return within a few years 'in opulence'. Indeed, for William Orr to be in India after all his misfortunes was considered a sure sign of the 'wisdom of Providence'. However, by the time Macartney's letter reached India early in 1807, William Orr had left Calcutta, as on the reverse of *A Vision,* it states 'left Calcutta Decr the 6th 1806, Arrived Peneng the 6th Jany 1807'. Macartney's letter was sent to an address in Calcutta but it was redirected to Penang.

WHYTEHALL NEAR BALLYMENA 31ST JULY 1806   *PRONI T/1956/7*

Sir

Your mother having yesterday shown me a letter from you to Mr Sam[l] Redmond and dated Calcutta January 28th 1806, under a name what the direct on this letter carries [*the letter is addressed to William Jamieson, watchmaker*]. I think it is necessary to say, that from a strict enquiry into the charge against you I found it was unfounded in truth, having proceeded from the most shameful malice established by the most infamous perjury. The result of my enquiry I communicated to Government, who sent orders to New South Wales to permit you to return to your country. This communication I make to you with great pleasure having been the magistrate who arrested you by order of the general of the district. Your brother John is with your mother at Creavery both well, I have great regard for them both & from your excellent character I have the same for you. I am happy to say that in the course of my enquiry about you I found that your advice instead of tending to promote rebellion in this country was of a very different complexion, having used your influence in dissuading the people from engaging in the foolish attempts, I assure you I was heartily sorry for your sufferings in consequence of the villainy of the artillery deserter, who was the cause of them by his unprincipled perjury, He died shortly after you left this country.

Your brother (when I called at your mother's house yesterday on my way here where I now reside having a put a curate into the Parish of Antrim) was on the point of going to Derry to settle with the friends of Mr Alexander the Hindostan Banker at Calcutta about remittances to you. However, I thought of a plan which will answer you better. I have written a letter, which I enclose to Councillor Stewart my nephew who is the head of his profession as a lawyer at Calcutta, who I have no doubt will be your friend in your business as a watchmaker. I advance what money you may want, I have mentioned £100. Your brother John will pay to Counsellor Stewart's mother at Ballytweedy near Antrim, what money he advances to you, immediately on his intimating the amount of the sum advanced.

I shall copy Lord Castlereagh's together with Mr Secretary Marsden's letter to me & the letter of the Under Secretary of State for Great Britain Mr King to Mr Marsden the Under Secretary here, from which you'l see that an order was sent to the Colonial Department for your enlargement, in order to your returning to your country.

If the climate agrees with you, I think you ought to remain in Calcutta, until you have realised what will make you comfortable for the remainder of your life & enable to assist your worthy mother. We are so short sighted that we often look on events which occur as misfortunes, which the wisdom of Providence intended for our good. In your case this observation applies in its' full extent, as your past sufferings promise greater advantages than you could have reap'd in your own country & the prospect of returning in a few years in opulence, where you will be higher in the esteem of all who have heard of you, than you would have been perhaps, had you been permitted to remain at home.

I am your friend & well wisher
    GEO. MACARTNEY

PS You may show this letter to Counsellor Stewart as my letter to him, so far as it relates to you, is confined to the money you may want.
[*Transcripts of the letters Macartney had received from Castlereagh, Marsden and King regarding the decision to allow Orr to return to Ireland are added to the letter*]
[*PostScript*] I enclose my letter to Counsellor Stewart in your brother's letter as it is lighter than this letter [*initialled*] GM

The reasons for William Orr's departure from Calcutta can only be speculated on. It was perhaps a perverse decision to leave a large city with ample opportunities for trade and commerce, for the small and remote colonial outpost of Penang. What may have unsettled Orr was the presence in Calcutta of two men who had been very much to the fore in Ireland. General Gerard Lake had achieved notoriety for the tactics he employed in disarming the United Irishmen of Antrim and Down during 1797 and had been insistent that William Orr be executed in Carrickfergus. In 1800 Lake was appointed Commander in Chief in India, where he led his forces to a string of stunning victories which promised to greatly expand British influence in India. Based in Calcutta, Lake remained in India until February 1807. If Lake's presence was unsettling to Orr, the parallels between India and Ireland must have become more striking in July 1805 when Lord Cornwallis arrived in Calcutta as Viceroy. Cornwallis had been appointed Lord Lieutenant in Ireland in June 1798 and it was on his initiative that a policy of pacification through conciliation was adopted rather than to rely on the punitive military polices of men such as Lake. Ironically, Cornwallis's mission in India was similar to that in Ireland, for he was required to rein in the activities of Lake. Although successful in battle, Lake's armies were costly to maintain and were not increasing the East India Company revenues. The Company directors in London were anxious that peace treaties be negotiated in North India rather than to continue with Lake's programme of conquest. While it is unlikely that the paths of either Lake or Cornwallis in Calcutta would have crossed Orr's, their very presence there may have been enough to convince him to leave. The final letter mentioned in *A Vision* as having been sent on 1 November 1806, could have signalled Orr's intention to leave Calcutta.[5]

CHAPTER 13 FOOTNOTES

1 William Jamieson, watchmaker, first appeared in the *East India Directory and Register* of 1808 (copies held in the India Office Library).

2 Letter from Rev. Macartney to William Orr (PRONI T/1956/7).

3 Malcomson (1972) *The extraordinary career of the 2nd Earl of Massereene, 1743-1805.*

4 Macartney letters regarding his son John: 28 March 1805 (PRONI D/572/16/78) and 16 Feb 1806 (PRONI D/572/16/127&128). A journal kept by John Macartney describing events in 1805-06 is in the British Library (BL MS C284). John Macartney died on 29 April 1811 at Meerut in India. He was 30 years of age.

5 *Dictionary of National Biography.*

14
Peter Pendulum, watchmaker

Penang or Poulo Penang is located about four miles from the north-west coast of the Malay peninsula. The island is small, about 15 miles long by 10 miles wide or roughly the same size as the Isle of Man. The western portion is mountainous with wooded hills rising to nearly 3000 feet but a fertile plain forms the east of the island. In 1786 the East India Company was seeking a base which would command the Straits of Mallacca and protect their main shipping route to China. Penang, with its sheltered anchorage and situation at the northern end of the Straits, was the ideal site and the Company was able to negotiate a lease on the island with the local King of Kedah. In addition to its strategic location, Penang offered the prospect of cultivating spices as well as expanding the Company's trading activities. The lease on the island was signed on the Prince of Wales's birthday (12 August 1786) and, in honour of this, the Company named their new possession Prince of Wales Island. Fortunately this name never achieved popular currency and private letters, such as Macartney's redirected letter to Orr and even the private correspondence of the Island's governors, inevitably referred to Pening or Penang.

The island thrived and it was raised to a full Presidency in 1805 by the East India Company with its own Governor and Council. By then the coastal plain had been settled with estates for the cultivation of pepper and nutmeg. Bungalows and a hospital had been built in the hills, where the European elite could escape from the heat and humidity of the plain. Although apparently un-populated in 1786, the population had grown to around 30,000, many of whom were living in Georgetown, the only town on the island which included Fort Cornwallis and Government House. Among the aims for the new colony, as set out by the East India Company in London, was that 'Farms were to be established for opium, arrack, gaming, tobacco, beetle leaf.' The Company's attitude to opium and gambling was equivocal. While it recognised that these gave 'encouragement to the most dangerous vices in society', the Company was prepared to take a pragmatic viewpoint especially if it could turn these vices to a profit – 'but we understand it has been thought that the Chinese and Malays being addicted to both [opium and gambling], it would not be practicable to effectually eradicate them & that under such circumstances it only remains to confine the indulgence in these propensities to particular parts of the town under such regulations and restrictions as would furnish a resource to government. But it would be far preferable in a political as well as a moral view, if these practices could be suppressed and we desire therefore that your attention may be directed to this end.' The referral to 'farms' meant that these activities would be licensed out under monopolies from which the Company would 'farm' the revenue. The Chinese love of pork was also exploited in a 'farm' for pig production. In addition to collecting customs, the Company maintained a monopoly in supplying ships' stores.[1]

Malays and Indians were the most numerous nationalities on the island but the large Chinese community operated many of the businesses in Georgetown, where there were also groups of Siamese, Burmese, Arabs and Armenians. The Europeans were mostly British with some of Portuguese extraction and a few Dutch. The male British contingent hardly exceeded 100 and could be divided into two groups. The Civil Establishment, employed by the East India Company, was headed by the Governor. The most famous of these was Sir Thomas Stamford Raffles, whose name lives on as Raffles Hotel in Singapore. The Governor ruled through an appointed Council and he had an accountant and store keeper who ensured that the Company was to make a profit on their investment in the Island. Law and order were enforced by a magistrate, police major and jailer. Altogether, 'Company Servants' numbered 60 plus a few soldiers who commanded the island's garrison. The remaining British, about 40 in number, were a diverse group, ranging from wealthy estate owners, living outside the town, to a few tradesmen, innkeepers and merchants operating in Georgetown. Among the latter was a sea captain, James G. Wilson who, in a letter to the Council in 1808, stated that he had only arrived in Penang in the summer of 1806 when he started to operate as a merchant, but before that he had been a sea-captain in India. This Captain Wilson may therefore have been the same individual who had taken William Orr from Sydney on the *Mersey*, which was an Indian built vessel. If so, it becomes probable that Wilson was Orr's point of contact in Penang and that Orr had followed him there in the winter of 1806-7.[2]

Records relating to William Orr's activities in Penang are scanty. From 1809, the *East India Directory and Register* began to list the European inhabitants of Prince of Wales Island and these lists included William Jamieson as a watchmaker. The minutes of the Council of the Island deal with weighty matters concerning the island's governance, and it is surprising therefore that they contain two references to William Jamieson. The impression these references give is that the riches which the Rev. Macartney imagined would come Orr's way were not to be easily realised. The first appeared in January 1808 in the form a letter sent to the island's Council.[3]

IOC G/34/19 p56-57

HONOURABLE GENTLEMEN, 11 JANUARY 1808

Having observed the irregular time give by the public clock in Fort Cornwallis since I have been resident in this island, and conceiving it to be of great utility to the inhabitants of the settlement that the public clock should at all times show the true time, I am induced to offer my services as watchmaker to keep the clock in constant repair and make it shew regularly the true time at this meridian, for which I trust the Honourable Board will take into account their consideration, that without some inducement to a person of my profession, the imoluments arising from the daily labour at present is barely adequate for subsistence, should the Honourable Board deem it an object worthy of attention whatever they may please to allow for such services will be gratefully acknowledged by their most obedient and humble servant.

WILLIAM JAMIESON

This request was successful for it is followed by the following entry in the minutes.

Resolved that Mr Jamieson be allowed the sum of 20 dollars per month from 1st of next month for keeping the Fort and Government House clocks in repairs.

COUNCIL CHAIRMAN COLONEL NORMAN MACALISTER.

The Spanish dollar was the common unit of currency in Penang, with an exchange rate of four dollars to the pound sterling, so Jamieson's income of $20 a month was modest and no passport to wealth and prosperity. By comparison, Penang's Governor received a surprisingly generous salary of $32000 plus a rent allowance of $4000. The secretary to the Council, accountant, surgeon and chaplain received salaries between $10000 and $6000. At the bottom of the scale, ten 'writers', the nineteenth century precursors of the word processor and photocopier, were each paid $120 per month.[4]

Four years later the Council received another letter as follows:

IOR G/34/34 P236-238

TO THE HONOURABLE GOVERNOR AND COUNCIL   5 MARCH 1812

Humble Sirs

I am impressed with the deepest sense of gratitude for encouragement I humbly beg leave to intrude myself upon your notice

Formerly when your Honourable Board was pleased to grant me the allowance of 20 dollars per month for keeping in repair the clock in the main guard, the then Honourable Governor was so good as to give me hopes that the allowance might in future be increased as circumstances should recommend.

It is allowed that a person of my profession is of much public convenience and while I exert my endeavours to be useful in the line of my business, I have to lament that (owing to the decreased state of the population) my imoluments from the publick is inadequate to my support.

May I therefore hope that your Honourable Board will be pleased to grant any addition to my present allowance which to your goodness may seem meet. With sentiments of the highest respect

W. JAMIESON

The minutes of the Council record a reply from the Governor of the Island.

> Impressed as I am with a sense of the respectability of the character and conduct of Mr Jamieson, it would be very gratifying to me to reward his honest and laudable industry by increasing his salary – if it would be done with propriety. I fear however that with reference to the services performed by him, the application contained in his letter cannot be complied with.

> A. SEFTON.

Jamieson's comment that his 'imoluments from the publick is inadequate to my support', might suggest he was not prospering. His reference to declining population refers to a downturn in Penang's economy for, after encouraging pepper production, there was an oversupply and prices fell accordingly. In addition the Napoleonic wars had an adverse impact on trade even in the Far East. It was the Secretary of the Council who usually replied to communications recorded in the Council's minutes, so it was most exceptional that the Governor of the Island, Archibald Sefton, a Scot, chose to reply in his own name. His tributes to Jamieson's 'respectability of character and conduct' and 'honest and laudable industry' are even more extraordinary. Sefton had many connections with Calcutta and, almost certainly, would have known Alexander Stewart, Macartney's nephew there. His comments suggests that he knew of William Jamieson's background and was paying tribute to his good behaviour.[5]

In 1816 William Jamieson was listed in the local newspaper, *Prince of Wales Gazette,* as having subscribed $10 to a fund to assist the dependants of soldiers killed at the Battle of Waterloo. Sixty individuals subscribed almost $3000, but Jamieson's was one of the more modest contributions and only nine were lower. This can be taken as more evidence of no great prosperity although, given his earlier politics, there may have been only a lukewarm enthusiasm towards the cause being subscribed to. However Jamieson began to diversify and, from 1819, he is listed as watchmaker and jeweller in the *East India Directory and Register.* An advertisement he placed in the *Prince of Wales Gazette* in 1817 was for the sale of 'A few cases of Hollands Gin'. The advertisement gave his residence as Beach Street in Georgetown.[6]

Beach Street, as its name implies, ran parallel to the sea and a drawing from the early 1800s shows fishermen's boats crowded behind the houses of Beach Street. It was the most built-up section of Georgetown but by no means a salubrious district. The papers of Stamford Raffles include a register of the 'Manilla Men, Portuguese etc. Inhabitants of Prince of Wales Island' which lists residents of Portuguese extraction, either from Portugal or from Portuguese colonies in Asia. Those resident in Beach Street were mostly fishermen, with some servants, a tailor, a shopkeeper and a lodging house keeper. More exotically there were three fiddlers and, not far from Beach Street in Love Lane, there was a 'Siamese Dancing Woman'. Also on Love Lane was another exotic dancer, Engah from Ceylon, who kept two slaves. In the same ledger Raffles recorded 135 prostitutes in Penang, 68 Malay and 67 Bengal. A petition from a few of the British residents to the Council complained that, because there were so many Chinese prostitutes in Georgetown, it was difficult for the poorer Chinese to find a bride. Houses in Georgetown were constructed to local standards with timber frames often slightly elevated on stilts to avoid flooding and roofs made of leaves. These houses were highly combustible and Georgetown, including parts of Beach Street, suffered devastating fires in 1808, 1812, 1814, 1815 and 1818. Epidemics were liable to sweep through the cramped quarters of the town, with cholera killing over 500 in three months of 1818 and returning with greater severity to claim almost 1000 over the winter of 1819-20.[7]

The *Prince of Wales Gazette* served as the local newspaper, carrying a few advertisements, Government announcements, records of shipping and rare snippets of local news. Its pages were filled out with extracts from the Calcutta, Madras and English papers and these columns of stale news depended on the arrival of ships from England and India. When there was a gap in arrivals the editor resorted to including extracts from books or poetry. In March 1818 he included the following poem.

EPITAPH ON A WATCHMAKER

Here lies in an horizontal position
The outside case of
Peter Pendulum, watchmaker
Whose abilities in that line, were an honor
To his profession.
Integrity was the mainspring
And prudence the regulator
Of all the actions of his life
Humane, generous and liberal

His hands never stopped turning
Till he had relieved a stress.
So nicely regulated were all his motions
That he never went wrong
Except when set a going
By people
Who did not know his key
Even then he was easily
Set right again
He had the art of disposing his time
So well
That his hours glided away
In one continual round
Of pleasure and delight
Till an unlucky minute put a period
To his existence
He departed this life
Wound up
In hopes of being taken in hand
By his Maker
And of being thoroughly cleaned and repaired
And set a'going
In the world to come.

The following edition of the *Prince of Wales Gazette* carried two so-called letters to the editor, so-called as the first letter could only have come from the editor himself, as it commented on a letter the editor had received in response to *Epitaph on a watchmaker.*

TO MR WILLIAM COX

EDITOR OF PRINCE OF WALES GAZETTE

Sir

Knowing that in the absence of intelligence from the Westward, you were last week rather in want of matter, and tenderly I sympathised with your editorial distress, I proceeded to examine the contents of my port folio in hope of being able to furnish you with as much as would at least fill half a column. In a search I stumbled upon the Epitaph on a watchmaker published in your last number copied from an old English magazine and is moreover highly complimentary in itself, I little thought it would cause so such animadversion or give the slightest offence to any of the craft. Judge therefore, Mr Editor my amazement and surprise, at receiving the accompanying choice scrap, which I request you will give to the public without a slightest change or amendment in the orthography or punctuation.

In the third paragraph the writer seems to have wound himself up to such a pitch as shews that his pen at least, if not his understanding, stands in need of regulation. But I am suddenly interrupted, for which in truth I am no means sorry as my hands are inclined to stop. Let me offer another epitaph which I trust will give no offence to any of our Cyclops or Vulcans for these are more formidable foes than my friend 'The Watchmaker'.

I am yours abruptly

Q__ P__ T___ S___

Pinang 13 March 1818.

The second letter then followed.

COMMENT ON THE EPITAPH ON A WATCHMAKER

About 15 months ago a coulored edditor of a Gazette obtained credit to a considerable amt of a Watchmaker Who after twelve months evasive procrastination found payment was not to be expected without legal means; instituted a process in Court to compel payment.

Mr Edditor in the fulness of his wrath or the workings of his malice has produced the sublime ferago entitled An Epitaph on a Watchmaker.

Thus it is that a Gazette supported by the Publick stoops to meanness of being the pander to private malice and the Engine for shooting the shafts of revenge.

A WATCHMAKER

There was only one watchmaker listed in Prince of Wales Island and that was William Jamieson. As the author of the letter from 'A watchmaker', Jamieson seems to have been sufficiently sensitive as to have interpreted the poem as an attack on himself. Evidently he had previously pressed a debt against 'a coloured editor', an Indian employed by Cox to produce the paper. Cox's letter perhaps carried a hint of threat in his phrase 'in need of regulation' while his referral to our Cyclops and

Vulcans suggests that he felt that the watchmaker had been needled into his riposte by others on the island.

In November 1821 William Jamieson announced his intention of leaving Penang with an advertisement in the *Prince of Wales Island Gazette*.

PRINCE OF WALES GAZETTE   NOV 28 1821

> Mr Jamieson begs leave to return his respectful thanks to the Public for the support he has experienced in a series of years; and as he intends proceeding to Europe by an early opportunity requests any claims against him will be presented for payments and those indebted to him will be pleased to discharge the same as early as possible.

The papers in the Creavery Orr collection in PRONI contain three letters on his departure from Penang. One is from the Police Office giving Mr Jamieson permission to leave the island on the ship *Amity*, which arrived in Penang on the 5 December 1821. The other two are from the Secretary to Council, the first requesting him to deliver over his charge of the Government Clocks, indicating that he was still drawing his salary for their care, and the second a favourable testimonial from the Governor of Prince of Wales Island. January 1822 saw William Orr on board the *Amity* and sailing home to Ireland as a free man. It had been 22 years since he had boarded the *Friendship* in chains to be banished from Ireland.

Letters on Orr's departure from Penang in 1821.

PRONI T/1956/8

[*on outside of folded sheet*] Mr William Jamieson

Prince of Wales Island Police Office the 15th December 1821 This is to certify that Mr William Jamieson has permission to quit this settlement and proceed to Europe in the ship Amity.

R ——————ty Superintendent of police

PRONI T/1956/9

[copy letter] No 745

MR WM. JAMIESON

Sir

I am directed by the Honourable the Governor in Council to desire that on your departure from this island, you will deliver over charge of the Government Clocks to J. Ruggill, who has been appointed to the care of them.

I am Sir
Your most obedient servant

    W. CLUBLEY
Secy to Gov.
Fort Cornwallis
The 14 December 1821

[copy letter] No 755

Sir

I am directed by the Honorable The Governor in Council to acknowledge the receipt of your letter of the 15 instant and to acquaint you that the Government has much satisfaction in testifying the highly favourable opinion they entertain of your conduct during the time you have resided at this Presidency and to add that in event of you wishing to return to India you may exhibit this testimony in your favour, with an assurance that it will highly advisable to comply with your wishes in that respect

I am Sir
Your most obedient servant

W. CLUBLEY SECY TO GOV.

Fort Cornwallis The 17 December 1821

CHAPTER 14 FOOTNOTES

1 For the origins of the Penang settlement see: a) index to East India Company Factory Records: Straits settlements -Malay Peninsular 1769-1830 (IOR G/34) and Mills (1925) *Penang 1786-1830*. Also map IOR X/3338. Walthen (1814) *Journal of a voyage in 1811 and 1812 to Madras and China* (p140) reported that its was dangerous to bathe near the shore in Georgetown on account of the alligators which are of 'a very large size'. Also mentions snakes of an 'enormous length' in the woods.

2 Letter setting up of presidency on Prince of Wales Island 18 April 1805 in *Dispatches to Prince of Wales Island* pp 1-115, (IOR G/34/186); Reference to opium etc pp63-65. Capt. Wilson references in IOR G/34/16 & 19.

3 It was only in 1809 that the *East India Directory and Register* (India Office Collection, British Library) first listed European residents of Penang. For Europeans, who were not part of the Company establishment, the lists given in the *Register* were somewhat out of date. William Jamieson only appears in Calcutta from 1808 and does not disappear from that list in 1815. The post of Clock-keeper was not a unique one in East India Company settlements for Ezekeil Fisk was Clock-keeper in Bencoolen and Fort Marlboro when Orr passed through there in 1804 (IOR G/35/45).

4 Letter setting up of presidency on Prince of Wales Island dated 18 April 1805 (IOR G/34/186, pp 1-115). Salaries of the Company establishment in 1805 were as follows. Council Members: Governor Philip Dundas ($32k + $4k rent allowance), Oliphant ($18k), Gray ($18k), Macalister ($18k). Lake (chaplain) $6.4k, Pearson (secretary) $8k, Hobson (accountant) $8k, Raffles (assistant secretary) $6k, Robinson $6k, William Dick (surgeon) $10k, Warring (assistant surgeon) $3k, Vacancy (assistant surgeon) $3k & 10 writers @ $1440. Total 26 staff. The regulations stated that the establishment civil servants listed above were not permitted to trade on their own account.

5 Background to Archibald Sefton (1755-1818) the son of Hugh Smith alias Sefton in IOR Neg. 11663-64.

6 *Prince of Wales Gazette* of June 1816 lists Penang subscribers for the relief of the British survivors who fell at Waterloo. Advert for sale of Hollands Gin *Prince of Wales Gazette,* 1 Feb 1817.

7 Bush & Rohatagi (1979) *Prints of South-east Asia in the India Office Library*. Raffles Collection Register of the Manilla men, Portuguese etc., inhabitants of Prince of Wales Island IOR E/110. Map of Georgetown shows areas which had experienced fires (IOC Map X/3345). *Prince of Wales Gazette* (25 Apr 1818) reported 4493 cases of cholera over a 9 week period of which 555 had died and 1173 convalescent. An entry in the Council minutes for 3 Feb 1820 (IOR G/34/74) gives a breakdown of deaths by racial origin from another cholera epidemic. Only one of the 974 deaths was a European. A comment by the surgeon on the island suggested that the total of 97 Chinese dead underestimated the actual death toll as the Chinese were under-reporting to avoid admitting the inferiority of Chinese medicinal approaches to treating cholera over European treatments.

15
An old Reformer is dead

William Orr was 48 years of age when he returned to Ireland in 1822. Despite his protestations of poverty in Penang, he had accumulated a sufficient store of wealth so as to set himself up in some comfort and was able to purchase Newgrove in Ballygarvey near Broughshane. Newgrove was probably a rather old-fashioned house even in the 1820s, as it had only a single storey and was thatched but, in size and comfort, it was well above the average farm house. It had been the home of the Duffin family and William Orr is believed to have found refuge there after his home at Creavery was burned in 1798. The Newgrove farm was also substantial by the standards of the Braid valley and extended to nearly 70 acres. He purchased land in the townland of Ballycregagh, a few miles to the north outside the village of Clough, and to the south he also owned land in Glenwherry. The lands at Ballycregagh and Glenwherry were let out to tenant farmers, so William Orr became a member of that much maligned species of mankind, an Irish landlord.[1]

He married Ellen Killen, who was some thirty years his junior. She was a daughter of John Killen, a Ballymena shopkeeper, and one of a family

A photograph of Newgrove circa 1890. The house survives now only as a garage behind the present day home of David Harkness who farms there.

of four boys and five girls. John Killen's wife was Martha Doole who, although born in Duneane, was brought up by her Millar uncles and aunts in Glenwherry. There are ill-defined but definite links between Duneane and the Orr family, while there is the story that William Orr of Farranshane,

The Avenue into Newgrove.

found refuge in Glenwherry in 1796 when he was on the run. However, there is little to connect any of Ellen Killen's relatives either to the Orrs or to the United Irishmen, except that John Killen was a distributor of the *Northern Star* in Ballymena in the 1790s.[2]

William Orr's years at Newgrove were unobtrusive with no indication that he either continued as a watch-maker or took part in the commercial life of Ballymena. His death on Christmas Day, 1860 at the age of 86, passed without comment or notice in the *Ballymena Observer.* He was buried in Kirkinriola burying ground where the headstone refers to the vicissitudes of his early life. There were no children from his marriage to Ellen Orr, to whom he left the house and farm at Newgrove. His other land was divided between the offspring of his brother John Orr of Creavery and his sisters, Eliza and Nancy. When Ellen Orr died eleven years later, she bequeathed Newgrove to a nephew, William Orr Wilson (1834-1906), a son of her sister Sarah and William Wilson, another Ballymena shopkeeper. William Orr Wilson had seven children but only four reached adult-hood: Major General Barnett Wilson (1862-1936), Rev. James Alexander Wilson (1872-1921), Blanche Brice Wilson (b1869) and Guy Wilson (1885-1962), who attained an international reputation as a breeder of daffodils.

By and large the story of their Uncle William's travels did not live long in the family memory and they seem largely lost to their late twentieth-century descendants. A letter sent by Major General Wilson in the 1930s gives but sketchy details. One of Ellen Orr's nephews was George Wilson who became a Presbyterian minister in Banbridge and London. In the 1930s two of his daughters, Margaret Lusk and Madeline Wilson, compiled a book dedicated to their father, who as a boy went to stay with his uncle and aunt at Newgrove. Aunt Orr apparently took delight in relating stories to her nephews which would send a shiver down their spines. However these yarns were not of her husband's travails, for all that is recorded by Margaret and Madeline is a reference to the skeletons of United men suspended in chains over the market house in Ballymena.[3]

What of the other Orrs? There were Orr farms in five townlands around Antrim in 1800, but by 1870 only Farranshane contained any Orrs. Today there are none, which hampers researches somewhat. The following notes on the Orrs of Farranshane, Kilbegs, Hurtletoot, Bleerick (The Folly), Creavery and Randalstown are therefore brief. Family trees presented in Appendix V are compiled from wills, census and land deeds but the information for many family lines does not extend far beyond the family trees produced by the Rev. Robert Magill at the end of the 1830s.

Mrs Isabella Orr, William Orr's widow, continued to live at Farranshane, bringing up a family of four girls and two boys. Her date of death is not known but it must have been after 1839, when Magill died and she was 71 years of age. William Orr's will divided the land at Farranshane between his two sons, with a proviso that the division would be into three parts if the youngest child, who had yet to be born when Orr was executed, turned out to be a son. The child was a fourth daughter, Wilhelmina, named after her father. Samuel, the eldest son, stayed on in the farm and married at the age of 25 in 1814, but ten years later he had died leaving two sons, James and William. The latter is likely to be the William Orr who is listed as farming in Farranshane in the post 1860 valuation records. He died in 1891, without making a will, and the farm passed to his son Samuel Orr who never married. On Samuel's death in 1928, Farranshane was bequeathed to Margaret Mulligan, a niece and Matt Orr, described in Samuel's will as a 'relative' and in the 1901 census form as a 'brother',

Farranshane 1999. William Orr's old home survives only as part of an out-house behind the present-day home of Sydney Montgomery.

but most likely a nephew born out of wedlock. Margaret Mulligan and Matt Orr lived together; she acting as housekeeper but the pair sold the farm during the 1939-45 war to Sam Montgomery of Marymount. Then the price paid for some 115 acres was but £1400, not a great deal more than the £800 Samuel Orr paid for it in 1779. The death of Matt Orr ended the Orr connection with Farranshane.[4]

The nocturnal floggings and arms seizures which had afflicted mid-Antrim in 1799 had ceased by 1801, by which time the political climate was solidly loyalist if not exactly pro-government. There can be no more telling indication of the changing allegiance of many in County Antrim than the career of Isabella Orr's second son John Orr who joined 42nd Royal Highland Regiment of Foot as an Ensign on 3 Oct 1811 aged 18. Today, his regiment is better known as the Black Watch and, ironically, it was one of the regiments which fought at Vinegar Hill in 1798. John Orr was promoted to Lieutenant in 1813 and he fought at Waterloo, where he was severely wounded and received the Waterloo medal. At the end of the Napoleonic Wars much of the British army was stood down and most officers placed on half pay, on condition they would serve again if called on. John Orr was still a Lieutenant when he was placed on half pay in March 1817 but he was then transferred to the 94th Regiment in August 1817, apparently on full pay. He then is listed as a half pay officer from December of that year but was paid from the Irish List, which paid Irish officer's pensions.

While most officers were retired on half pay, a small proportion received full pay on their retirement. In 1820, John Orr was granted retirement on full pay and was listed as a member of the 8th Royal Veteran Battalion – all officers retired on full pay were listed under the eight Royal Veteran Battalions. As a civilian, John Orr continued to work for the army as a barrack master in Ireland. The barrack master was responsible for ensuring that troops were kept supplied with provisions and in this capacity John Orr served in Clonmel (County Tipperary), Longford, Birr or Parsonstown (County Offaly) before ending up as barrack master of the Royal Barracks in Dublin in the 1840s. In terms of salary and responsibilities, this was, along with Cork, the most senior barrack master post in Ireland, with an annual salary of £274. In addition to being responsible for the Royal Barracks, Orr's duties extended to Dublin barracks in Ship Street, Aldborough House and Mountjoy. John Orr sold his interest in Farranshane in 1859 and was residing in Edinburgh when he died on 7 Dec 1879, by which date he was one of the few surviving soldiers who had fought at Waterloo.[5]

James Orr of Cranfield had made frantic attempts to save his brother William in 1797. Throughout the 1790's he continued to hold the position of High Constable for the Barony of Upper Toome. In the spring of 1800, the Antrim County Grand Jury minute book records a resolution that the Grand Jury would take direct control the appointment of Constables in the various baronies of County Antrim. James Orr was an early casualty of this policy, for by the summer he had been replaced by 'Black Sam' Feniston of Brecart, who had fought as a yeoman in the Battle of Antrim. James died, aged 44, in 1814. He had married three times but only one son, William Orr survived to adulthood. This William became a leading solicitor in Ballymena and, like his father before him, made a 'good' marriage, marrying Mary Harrison, a member of a prominent Ballymena family. William Orr eventually took over the Harrison home at Hugomount on the outskirts of Ballymena. He maintained an interest in the wider Orr family and acted as their solicitor and, in 1859, purchased for £1100 the half interest in the townland of Farranshane from his cousin Lieutenant John Orr.[6]

This William Orr had a large family of 11 children when he died in 1873. At least some of his sons were sent to English public schools. Two achieved high rank in the army, while three others entered the legal profession. John Orr QC became a County Court judge and died in Dublin in 1920. Hugh Harrison Orr was a solicitor in Australia, while Robert Harrison Orr continued on in his father's business as a solicitor, although based primarily in Belfast, rather than Ballymena. Robert had two sons, one of whom, Capt. Robert Clifford Orr, was killed in action in 1914. The other son, William J.J. Orr followed his father as a solicitor in Belfast until his death in 1952 at his home in Craigavad.

The youngest brother of William Orr of Farranshane was Samuel of Kilbegs. He died in 1831 and, according to the *Ordnance Survey Memoir*, was in Carrickfergus jail at the time for debt. His wife, Mary Redmond survived him by six years. She had been 32 when she married him but had produced ten children, three of whom died young. Magill's genealogy shows that all but one of the seven survivors emigrated to America. The exception was Joseph Orr who took over the farm on his father's death. Joseph had married by then and had six children before his wife died in 1835. It seems that he married again, this time to Jemina Orr, a second cousin and the daughter of John Orr of Creavery. They had a further four children. What became of Joseph's large family of 10 children is unknown.

No Orrs were recorded at Kilbegs in the Griffiths valuation of 1860 and neither is there any record of a will for Joseph Orr. In 1878 Jemina Orr was described as a widow with a Belfast address. One of her sons, James, was listed then as a compositor.[7]

The fate of John Orr of The Folly remains in doubt but there is no indication that the death sentence he received at his court martial was ever carried out. Given his age, there is a possibility that he died in prison. Magill lists only three children, including two sons Samuel and James. Samuel lived at Harp Hall in Hurtletoot, which was burned in 1798, and it was there that he died in 1807, leaving his wife to rear five children. Samuel's son John Orr married his cousin Wilhelmina Orr in 1819. After ten years of marriage and two children, Magill records that the couple separated and that John had gone to America having 'sold his seat' in the Mill Row church. Wilhelmina was presumably left to sit with her mother but, some twenty years later, she married John Moorehead. In the 1830s no Orrs were in Hurtletoot. James Orr was the other son of John Orr of The Folly and he continued to live there and raise a family. From valuation records he was succeeded by his eldest son John who died around 1860, apparently without any issue, for in the valuation lists he is succeeded by his older sister, Fanny. Within a few years of this, the farm at the Folly was in the hands of an Alexander Thompson.[8]

The drinks that John Orr of Creavery stood for Wheatley and Lindsay that April evening in Antrim could be considered as the pebbles which set off an avalanche which was to engulf the Orrs. Indeed, one can but speculate on the course of history, not only for the Orrs but of Ulster, if the two fencibles been allowed to go on their way. After fleeing to America in July 1798, John Orr had by 1806 been able to return to Antrim, when Macartney visited Creavery. In that year he married Jane Darragh who bore him six girls and a son, William who died at the age of 11 from consumption. For the remainder of his life, John Orr lived on his farm in Creavery. The house, which had been burnt in 1798, was rebuilt and by the 1830s, when the First Poor Law Valuation of property was undertaken, it was the largest of the Orr properties recorded. After his death in 1840, the farm was sold.[9]

John Paul of Tobernaveen had been a neighbour of the Creavery Orrs in the 1790s, but was rather younger than them, being twenty-one years of age in 1798. Forty-five years later Paul claimed that he, 'almost alone' of his boyhood friends, neighbours and relatives, had resisted 'the tide of public opinion, sweeping all before it' to join the Union of United Irishmen.

Creavery House in the early 1880s, when it was occupied by the Kirk family.

Creavery House in 1999. It is the home of Crawford and Ruth Dennison and their family. The dimensions of the house seem to be those of the house present at the time of the first Poor Law Valuation in 1833.

By this time, John Paul was minister to the scattered societies of Covenanters living in the hills that stretched from Lough Mourne, above Carrickfergus, southwards to Carnmoney. Within the spectrum of beliefs which made up nineteenth-century Irish Presbyterianism, the Covenanters' wavelength was radically different from the New Light Presbyterians, and Paul was a fierce polemicist against them. But like many Presbyterians he was a liberal in political outlook. In 1840, when William Orr of Newgrove asked John Paul to write an obituary to his brother, John Orr, Paul felt no embarrassment in honouring an old United Irishman who had retained his attachment to the principles of civil and religious liberty. While we may ponder how long John Orr endured 'petty annoyances' for his political beliefs, John Paul's lines bring to an end this account of the Orrs of Antrim.[10]

PRONI T/1956/11

AN OLD REFORMER

It is our painful duty to record the death of an old Reformer John Orr Esq. of Creavery near Antrim. He departed this life in the 5 inst. in the 70th age of his age.

Mr Orr was no ordinary man. He was possessed of a powerful, active and discriminating mind – he was endued with great firmness & decision of character. Few men understood so well, or loved so ardently or promoted so zealously the principles of civil & religious liberty. He embraced them early & clung to them through good & bad report. His attachment to those principles cost him dear. Persecutions, spoilations & petty annoyances were the price he paid but none of these things moved him.

He lived and died as an implacable enemy of tyranny & despotism. Expressing his trust & hope in the Saviour he expired in the bosom of his amiable & affectionate family, exhorting them to the exercise of a similar dependence.

CHAPTER 15 FOOTNOTES

1 The will of William Orr of Newgrove and Griffiths valuation for Ballymena Poor Law Union (PRONI)

2 Killen (1901) *Reminiscences of a long life*. pp 1-14.

3 Kenny (1988) *As the crow flies over rough terrain*. pp 152-170 & 186-187.

4 A transcript of the will of William Orr of Farranshane is given in Appendix IV. In addition to Magill's Names of seat-holders, the records of land holdings held in PRONI through the Tithe Applotment lists of 1833 (FIN/5A/13), the First Poor Law Valuation of 1836 (VAL/1b/16) and the Second (Griffiths) Poor Law Valuation of 1860 (VAL/2B/1/5A) and subsequent Revision Note-books (VAL/12B/1a-d & 2a-b) provide details of changes in ownership and tenancies in the five townlands. In the 1830s, Isabella Orr and her daughter-in-law Matilda Orr (Widow Samuel Orr) lived in Farranshane, but in separate houses. The houses were each valued at £3 annual rental in 1836, but this value was reduced by 5% 'for close neighbourhood'. Farranshane was then a clachan type settle- ment with perhaps as many as 8 houses plus labourers' cottages. In the 1830s only Isabella seems to have a direct interest in land with 10 acres out of the 112 acres in the townland. Her daughter-in-law made do with half an acre. By 1860, William Orr, probably Matilda's son, was in residence but only farmed 13 acres leased from a John Gilmour. By 1880, most of the other tenants present in 1860s had gone to be replaced by a Samuel Orr as well as William Orr. The remaining land was farmed by a William Orr Wilson, who may have been a grandson of William Orr, through his daughter Isabella's marriage to William Wilson. Frederick Orr Mulligan received a small legacy from his Uncle Samuel Orr in 1929 and he is the only other name to be recorded on the headstone to Ally Orr in Templepatrick. It is said that Fred Mulligan had collected much material relating to the Orrs but that his sister Margaret Mulligan burned it when he died.

5) John Orr. The annual *Army Lists* (held in PRO, London) give 4 John Orrs (1 Lieuten- ant Col, 1 Major and 2 Lieutenants) as officers during the first two decades of the 19th century. The first two of these men cannot have been John Orr of Farranshane as he would have been too young when they first held rank in the Army. The other Lieut. Orr died too early (pre 1850) to be John Orr of Farranshane. The remaining John Orr's army career is summarised in the House of Commons Sessional Paper 1821(129)xi.113. John Orr's changing residencies can be traced from title deeds concerning his ownership of his inheritance at Farranshane (Reg. of Deeds 1843/36/17; 1844/11/24 & 1859/4/1). The last of these in 1859 refers to him as resident in the Royal Barracks, Dublin. He had been barrack master there from at least 1847 (see references to John Orr in Dublin in House of Commons Sessional Papers 1847(169)xxxvi.32, 1847-48(553)xli.479 and 1849(499)ix.5). The first of these references specifically states that he had held the rank of Lieutenant in the army. Despite this in *Slater's Directory* of 1856 he is listed as Capt. Orr, Barrack Master of the Royal Barracks, Dublin. The *New Annual Army List* of 1840 (held in PRONI) mentions that Orr was severely wounded at Waterloo. Bigger's promotion of John Orr to Major Orr is therefore improbable, as is his account of Orr's renouncing his allegiance to the army prior to discharge after Waterloo, given his favourable treatment in receiving a pension and the fact that the rest of Orr's working life was spent serving the army.

6) County Antrim Grand Jury Presentment Books (PRONI ANT/4/2/7/1) and Grand Jury Resolution Book 1780-1824 (PRONI ANT4/7/1). A resolution passed in Lent 1800 stated that 'names [of constables] to be submitted to full Grand Jury in point of character'. At

The Orr headstone in Templepatrick. Although dozens of Orrs must have been buried in the graveyard there is only this headstone dedicated to Ally Orr. Almost certainly, given the lack of weathering and continuity of style in the two inscriptions, it replaces an earlier headstone dedicated to Ally Orr. In front of the headstone is the memorial erected by the *Remember Orr Commemoration Committee* in 1998.

the next Grand Jury meeting in the summer of 1800 Sam Feniston appeared as a replacement for James Orr.

7) Day & McWilliams (1995) *Ordnance Survey of Ireland. Parishes of Co. Antrim XI.* p 7. The marriage of Jemina Orr to Joseph Orr is somewhat speculative. In the will of William Orr of Newgrove (1856), Jemina is described as of Kilbegs and as having children, but there is no mention as to who her husband was. In 1879, when she sold her inheritance received from William Orr she is described as a Jemina Orr, widow (Reg. of Deeds 1878/11/288). My opinion that she was the wife of Joseph Orr is strengthened by the fact that none of her four children listed in this deed had the Christian names of any of the children from Joseph Orr's first marriage.

8) Antrim Poor Law Valuation notebooks.

9) John Orr's home was valued in 1836 at a rental of £7-15-1 compared to £7-9-11 for the Orr home in Kilbegs. There was a considerable amount of farm buildings attached to the farm at Creavery but the assessor considered that 'there are a greater number of houses on this farm than required, about 1/4 are unusable and might be disposed with'. By the time of this valuation John Orr was a fairly old man of 67 and had evidently scaled down his farming activities. He died 5th June 1840 (PRONI T/1956/11), but there is no headstone to John Orr. There is a memorial in Carmavy Graveyard, off the Seven Mile Straight, to his eldest daughter, Eliza, who married Isaac Kirker of Carnaghliss. Their children benefited from the estate of William Orr of Newgrove, in whose will Isaac Kirker is described as William's friend and was appointed an executor. This Kirker headstone fractured and collapsed face-downwards in 1998, but is recorded in *Carmavy Graveyard 1993*. The chronology of Eliza's death in *Carmavy Graveyard* does not seem correct as it infers she pre-deceased her husband, but the headstone states that she had erected it in memory of her husband. William Orr, the only son of John Orr and Jane Darragh, is commemorated in the headstone to his Darragh grandparents in Connor Graveyard (see: Allen & Gaston (1995) *Inscriptions at St Saviours Parish Church, Connor*).

10) See McCollum (1994) *The life of John Paul*. The obituary does not seem to have been published. Attached to the obituary is the following letter: 'Wm. Orr Esq., Newgrove, Ju 10 1840. My Dear Sir, I send you a few lines which I promised. If nothing better is offered have the goodness to accept them as a small tribute of respect to the memory of your brother. I am dear Sir your sympathising friend. John Paul, C.fergus, May [sic?] 10, 1840.'

Appendix I

Colonel Clavering's Proclamations

The following are transcripts of proclamations issued by Col. Clavering on the 8, 9 and 10 June 1798 ordering and threatening the Rebels if they did not surrender after the Battle of Antrim. They are from originals in the National Library of Ireland and State Archives of Ireland.

The first document is a covering letter sent by Clavering to Brigadier General Knox who was the army commander in the area to the west of Lough Neagh arranging a rendezvous between Clavering and Knox's forces who were marching from South Derry to County Antrim.

NLI 56/P185

SHANE'S CASTLE
8 JUNE 1798

Col Clavering to General Knox

My Dear Sir

You will be already in possession of the circumstances of yesterday [the Battle of Antrim]. Col Durham returned with the Monaghan Regt and his detachment of Dragoons to Belfast. I proceeded to towards Randalstown in information that the Rebels occupied it. On our approach at a miles distance they fled in all directions towards Toome. We recovered some yeomen prisoners with the guard set over them who are now in custody. A letter which the enclosed proclamation will explain was given me this morning. I shall march tomorrow morning at day break to Randalstown and burn the place if the terms held out are not complied with, which you will be enabled to judge by the appearance of the fugitives with or without arms. If they are delivered an express shall be forwarded you to that intent. Should the Rebels not appear in force to oppose us I have General Nugent's orders to return to Blaris leaving two hundred infantry, including Antrim Yeomanry and troop of the 22nd Dragoons to garrison Antrim and to desire you in his name to return to Dungannon. In either case intelligence shall be sent to you. The County of Down is apparently quiet and it is my opinion the insurgents will not stand against the army. I have the honor to be my Dear Sir & Yours truely

W. CLAVERING

Since writing and sealing this letter I understand an arch of Toome Bridge
has been broken down therefore dispatch by Lurgan

Clavering's Proclamation (below) was attached to above letter

NLI 56/p186

PROCLAMATION

8 JUNE   SHANE'S CASTLE

Col Clavering Commanding his Majesties Forces in and about Antrim
and armed with full and sufficient powers to crush the Rebellion, has
received a letter addressed to Mr James Dickey, Randlestown, wherein it
is expressed 'That if he can treat with Mr Jones and engage that there
shall be no more disturbance we (meaning those in arms) in opposition to
his Majesties forces will comply but that if he Mr Jones does not insure
that there shall be no person here (in Randlestown) molested, we will
take care of the prisoners and if he (Mr Jones) makes a sure engagement
we will release the prisoners now in hand and become as we were
formerly.'[1]

In answer to which Col. Clavering desires it may be intimated to these
unfortunate persons, who have been seduced from their true allegiance to
his Majesty King George the third, That if they will return to their duty as
faithful subjects to the Crown and to their respective trades and
occupation, he does hereby surely engage that no-one whatever in this
country shall be molested or their property injured, and that as proof of
their return to Loyalty they must in course of this night liberate their
prisoners and send them to Castle Shane and pile all their arms whether
guns, pikes or offensive weapons by whatever name known with their
ammunition on the high road between Randlestown and Antrim at one
mile distant from the former place, which the Kings troops will take
possession at an early hour to-morrow morn, And at the same time release
all prisoners in their custody,

But if the insurgents do not comply with the above injunctions Col
Clavering assures them most positively he will to-morrow set fire to and
totally destroy Antrim, Randalstown and every town, village and farm
house in the county and put everyone to the sword without form of tryal
whatever. He earnestly entreats them therefore and conjures them in the

name of humanity of everything they hold most dear, to prevent such effusion of blood and total destruction of all property and trade.

The following two proclamations, written after Randalstown had been burned, offered the Rebels in Ballymena terms for their surrender.

REB. PAPERS 620/38/99

Copy

SHANE'S CASTLE 9TH JUNE 1798

Colonel Clavering commanding His Majesty's Forces in and about Antrim, has rec^{d.} a letter dated this day from Ballymena signed Messrs McClaverty & Neile McPike stating that they are required & authorised by the people in arms, to say they accept the terms in the proclamation and as proof thereof send the prisoners taken at Randalstown & also all arms and ammunition together with the other prisoners now in custody at Ballymena shall be surrendered at any hour & place Colonel Clavering may appoint and they are also authorised to say that upon these terms they will return to their homes in peace and quietness and in dutiful allegiance. Colonel Clavering therefore in full compliance that the unfortunate persons who have been seduced will as Men and Irishmen be true and faithful unto their word has released the prisoners confined in Shane's Castle and he does hereby direct that all arms, pikes or offensive weapons and ammunition of every description must be brought on carrs to Shane's Castle this evening before seven o'clock and the persons to whom they belong must disperse and return to their respective habitations, and as Clavering has rec^{d.} positive information that the force assembled at Ballymena consists of upwards of 2000 persons each of whom can bring into the field five more completely armed he desires it may be fully understood that the arms and ammunition be sufficient for 10000 that is of arms including all descriptions, and further that Mr Dickey of Crumlin must be given up at the same time with all prisoners confined at Ballymena, on these conditions and these only Colonel Clavering assures to all persons of this county who have been engaged in the late conspiracy to subvert the Laws and Constitution of Ireland, a full pardon on their giving their names to Messrs Wm. McClaverty & Neile McPike who in order to prevent any unfortunate reflection on and consequences to the persons concerned should be publickly known are hereby authorised and directed to take a solemn oath on the Holy Evangelist never to reveal the names of any unarmed except in a Court of

Justice in cases when the persons now returning to their allegiance may be accused of having formerly engaged in treasonable practices, when the declarations of said Messrs McClaverty & Neile McPike shall free them from any prosecution for any seditious practices they may have been concerned in person to this day.

Signed W.H. CLAVERING COL.

I pledge myself that if the above Dickey is given up he shall not be brought before any military tribunal but his case shall be submitted to a fair and impartial jury of his countrymen.

W. H. CLAVERING COLONEL

We do certify that the above is a true copy this 10th June 1798.
Signed

WM. M. McCLAVERTY, NEAL McPIKE

Copy   SHANE'S CASTLE 10TH JUNE 1798

On account of the appearance of returning tranquillity in the County, Colonel Clavering pledges himself that if the arms are brought in to him from all quarters without delay both by day and night & neither the person or property of any individual shall be molested & if from any unforeseen accident any person shall be injured in his property, Colonel Clavering pledges himself to indemnify them on their making affidavit before a magistrate of the value thereof. Mr Dickie and Mr Smith are authorised to circulate the above
Signed

W. H. CLAVERING

FOOTNOTES

1 The Mr Jones referred to may have been Thomas Morres Jones, a landlord and magistrate of Moneyglass House, near Toome, whose son Thomas Hamilton Jones had been taken prisoner by the Rebels in Randalstown. Mr James Dickey, who the Rebels chose to communicate with, lived at Hollybrook near Randalstown. The Dickey's owed their wealth to linen and the mills they operated in Randalstown. It is not clear what connection there was, if any, between this James Dickey and James Dickey, the attorney of Crumlin who was executed in Belfast. It does seem strange however that the Crumlin Dickey chose to be in Randalstown on the 7th June 1798.

2 Clavering's offer of, what amounts to, a general amnesty was noted by Dr Magee who had been in Randalstown and who later became an informant of Madden. Magee bitterly referred to what he regarded as Clavering's treachery in subsequently burning Randalstown after arms had been given up. However Magee and Madden make no mention of the additional requirement to give up prisoners as well as arms. (*Antrim & Down in '98* p60).

Appendix II
Samuel Orr's compensation claim

Samuel Orr submitted this compensation claim for property losses he suffered in 1798. It shows that, in addition to his home at Kilbegs, which was burned in June 1798, Orr also owned a house about 8 miles away in the Parish of Duneane which was also burned. The first two sections of the claim cover the rebuilding costs of both the houses and their associated outhouses. The final section covers the house contents which were destroyed along with farm implements. The inventory gives a glimpse of the standard of living which the Orrs had achieved. They also provide evidence of a dual currency system being used in Ulster at least. In 1799 the £ in Ireland was worth less than the £ sterling used in England & Scotland with an exchange rate of 13 for 12 so it took 13 Irish pennies to make one English shilling. Most furniture items seem to have been originally priced in English guineas (21 shillings) or parts of guineas. These were then converted to Irish pounds shillings and pence.[1]

CONVERSION TABLE FOR ENGLISH GUINEAS AND CROWNS
TO IRISH POUNDS

1 Guinea	=	21s sterling (Stg.)	=	£1 2s 9d Ir.
° Guinea	=	10s 6s Stg.	=	11s 4°d Ir.
1° Guinea	=	£1 11s 6s Stg.	=	£1 14s 1°d Ir.
2 Guineas	=	£2 2s Stg	=	£ 2 5s 6d Ir.
3 guineas	=	£3 3s Stg.	=	£ 3 8s 3d Ir.
5 guineas	=	£5 5s Stg.	=	£ 5 13s 9d Ir.
6 guineas	=	£6 6s Stg.	=	£ 6 16s 6d Ir.
° crown	=	2s 6d	=	2s 8°d Ir.
1 crown	=	5s	=	5s 5d

Estimate of repairs to be made to Saml Orrs house in Toome,
Parish of Duneane & County of Antrim.

	£	s	d
To roofing 52 feet 6 inches by 34 feet over being 17 squares Timber and sleat	53	11	
To parlour flooring & joining & ceiling at £3 per square being 3 floors 8 squear &54 feet at £2 10s.	22	15	
Do 2 floors 22 feet by 20 feet at £2 10s per squear	22	15	
Over cellars 3 floors 22 feet by 12 8 squears	20		
Little room 10 feet by 18 @ Do	3		
4 sashes 6 by 3:6 trimmed etc @ 2s per foot	8	16	
17 Upper sashes 4 feet by 2:6	17	10	
Hall door etc	1	10	
6 framed do iner side	12		
freestone chimney pieces in parlour	2	5	6
5 outher Do	2		
To Brick partions puled down and carried away	5		
To Cut stoane stears at hall door & window stools	11	18	
To Door & window arckitrives	1	2	9
To Stear case etc	6	16	6
To 21 window shutters framed work	10		
To Plaster & cealing 98 yards	4	18	0
	207	17	9

Stables etc

	£	s	d
To 48 feet by 24:5 over roofing	25	17	6
To 4 outer doors and one inner doore etc	2		
To 4 window frames	9	2	
To Joining & flooring 31 by 15 wide	9	2	
To Little house appart 15 by 15 flooring etc	4	13	
To 31 feet long rack and meanger	4	10	
	254	8	3

Estimate of repairs to be maid to Saml Orrs house in Killybegs,
Parish & County of Antrim which was burned & destroyed in time
of the Troubles in this Country in June 1798.

	£	s	d
Roofing 15 squares & 30 feet @ £2 6s 6d	35	11	5 °
Slateing 17 squares & 30 feet @ £1 15s 0d	30	5	6

	£	s	d
15 large windows framed sashed trimed & glazed @ £2	30	0	
2 smaller ditto the same @ 18s ft	1	16	
Arckatrives & shutters framed work to ditto	15	11	3
Hall door & case	5	5	
Kitchen door & case	1	14	1 °
Studing lathing & plastering 52 yds partitions	5	4	
4 squares & 60 feet flooring @ £2 ?s	11	10	
15 squares & 20 feet ditto @ £2	30		
Lathing & plastering ceilings 169yds @ 1s 6d	12	19	6
Plastering walls 444 yds @ 1s	22	4	
A stair case four flights @ £3	12	0	
Kitchen grate and crane	4	0	
seven small graits	5	13	9
No 1	**233**	**16**	**7**

A small house at the end of the large one

	£	s	d
Roofing & covering six squares @ 15s	4	10	
A doore and case		15	
2 small windows fraimed sashed and glazed	1	2	
Plastering walls of do 40 yds @ 9d	1	10	
A board partition through said house	2	5	6
No 2	**10**	**2**	**6**

A cowhouse and potato house & store

	£	s	d
Roofing and covering 21 squares @15s	15	15	
4 Doores and doore cases	3	0	
A revallree and stalls [?] for 10 cows	3	0	
No 3	**21**	**15**	

A baron and stable

	£	s	d
Roofing and covering 24 squares @15s	18	0	
4 Doores and doore cases	3	0	
Recks and mangers	5	0	
No 4	**26**	**0**	

	£	s	d
No 1	233	16	7
No 2	10	2	6
No 3	21	15	0
No 4	26	0	0
Total of house repairs	**291**	**14**	**1**

**An inventory of goods taken and destroyed between the 7th
and 12th of June last by his majesties forces in said house**

	£	s	d
??????	6	16	6
A clock case and weights	4	16	3
A short posted beadsted and hanging	3	0	0
A mahoganey dineing table	3	0?	0?
A marble side table	2?	5	6
A bead beadsted and beadding	12	1	6
A beason stand		11	4 °
A dressing table		8	1 °
A looking glass	1	2	9
One sett of mahoganey chest of drawers	5	2	4 °
One dining table Oval	1	14	3
A large press	2	5	6
Six oake chaires	1	16	
A beadsted and hangings	5	19	7
A cupboard and wall cove		16	3
A cloathes chest	1	7	3
An oake chest of drawers	2	16	1 0 °
Two firr chairs		5	5
A bead and beadsted	3	8	3
An other ditto	3	16	4 °
An other ditto	2	5	6
A chest of drawers firr	1	13	0
A kitchen table		6	6
A hanging dressor		5	5
Two punchens of oatmeal seeds	3	16	1 0 °
Sixteen pecks of groats	2	8	0
Six chairs	1	2	9
A dining table beech		5	5
Timber	2	5	6
five tuns of oat meal & £12	60	0	
Twenty five hundred oatmeal seeds @ 6s 6d	8	2	6
Two meale arkes	3	16	10
Two carrs	6	3	0
Three carrboxes and reckes	2	10	0
Ploughing utensils and ploughs	2	15	1 1 °
Sacks and winnowing cloath	4	18	6
Saddles and bridles	6	0	11

	£	s	d
A pillion	1	2	9
Wheat and oats	19	0	
Six cowes	42	0	
	£234	09	9 °

Inventory of goods continued

	£	s	d
Brought over	234	9	9 °
Two horses	25	0	0
Turff	2	5	6
One set of Northumberland tables	3	0	
One dozn oake chairs	3	5	
One boffet	1	14	1 °
One looking glass	4	0	
A stand table	1	2	9
An oak desk	4	11	
A chest of drawers mahoganey	2	5	6
One oake ditto	5	13	9
A looking glass		11	4 °
A boffet	1	0	
A beadsted	2	15	10 °
A press	1	14	1 °
A kitchen table		14	1 °
A dresser	1	6	10 °
Six fir chairs		16	5 °
One table		5	0
Five joynt stooles & small chairs		9	
Four water canns		13	
A creadle		11	4 °
A bench and gaw tub		13	
A salt chest		5	5
Gleaks shelves and salt box		13	
A large washing tub	1	14	1 °
A churn and butt	1	14	1 °
A small churn and butt		19	
Milch vessals		19	6
one and a half dozn nogins		6	6
Four tea kettles	1	15	9
Five candlesticks		16	10
A corner cupboard of fir deal		16	3
12 puter plates and 8 large dishes	1	6	9 °
Delph wair	3	0	0
Pots gridiron & frying pan	1	3	8

	£	s	d
Three sets of fire irons	1	8	8
One large chest of oak and pantry shelves	1	2	9
Two & half dozn knives and forks	1	10 4	°
A knife box		2 8	°
Wooden dishes		12	
A bake board bowle		5	11
Two spinning wheels & a reel	1	5	
Total sum of the inventory	**£320**	**15 9**	**°**

Total sum of house repaires & inventory

	£	s	d
Page first house repaires	291	14	1
Pages secd and third inventory	320	15 9	°
Total sum is	**612**	**91 0**	**°**
Amount of repairs to Dunin Toome house	254	8	3
Total amount in all	**£866**	**18**	**3**

I, Saml Orr of Kilbegs in the County of Antrim do swear that I have
sustained losses in the late rebellion to the amount eight hundred & sixty
six pounds & eighteen shillings & three halfpence sterling as appears by
the foregoing acct and that the foregoing account estimates are just and
fair and that there not too great a value set upon any article in said
account to the best of my knowledge and belief.

SAML ORR

Sworn before me at Antrim in the County of Antrim this 8th day of April
1799.

JACKSON CLARK

FOOTNOTE

1 The burning of the house at Duneane is referred to in a letter sent by Capt. W.H. Snowe
from Moneymore to General Knox, in which Snowe had to state the number of houses
he had burned, He admitted to only two in County Antrim, one described as Orrs and the
other as Hendersons. (NLI MSS 56/p203).

Appendix III

Transcript of the court martial
of John Orr 15 November 1798

REB. PAPER 620/17/17

Proceedings of a General Court Martial held in Belfast on 15th day of Nov. 1798 by order of Major General Goldie.

PRESIDENT:	Major Anderton	Lancashire Light Dragoons
MEMBERS:	Capt. Scott	64th Regiment
	Capt. James	Monaghan Regiment
	Capt. Cary	64th Regiment
	Capt. Barbor	Lanc. Light Dragoons
DEPUTY JUDGE ADVOCATE:	Lieut. Whiteway	Lancashire Light Dragoons

To try such Prisoners as may be brought before them.
The Court being duly sworn proceeded to the Trial of John Orr of The Folly near Antrim.

CHARGE:

> For that **John Orr** is a Treator and a Rebel to our Sovereign Lord the King and that he did on 7th day of June last at Antrim in the County of Antrim and at several other times and places command divers Acts of treason and Rebellion against our said Lord the King by exciting, threatening and forcing divers liege Subjects of our said Lord the King to join him in Rebellion which then existed within this Kingdom. And that he the said John Orr as a false Treator and Rebel to our said Lord the King, did on the said 7th day of June on the County of Antrim aforesaid appear in Arms and did take upon himself the Command of a number of Armed Men and acted as their Commanding Officer against the peace of our said Lord the King his Crown and Dignity.

> To which charge the Prisoner pleaded **Not Guilty**.

EVIDENCE:

Henry O'Hara being duly Sworn says he knows the Prisoner. That on the 7th day of June last he saw him in the Neighbourhood of the Town of Antrim at the head of between 20 and 30 Men armed some with Guns, Pikes and Pitchforks, & the Prisoner was also armed and desired the party of whom he appeared to have the Command to burn the Houses of such as would not join them, further says that on the road to Temple Patrick they met a man who was going orderly from another party of Rebels, who the Prisoner stopped, who desired the Prisoner to proceed with his Party on to Antrim which he accordingly did and when within about a mile of the Town Witness heard the Prisoner give the orders for the young Men to go in front. The Prisoner in conversation with Witnesses on the Road informed him that he the Prisoner had sat up all the night before making pike shafts.

QUESTION BY PRISONER:

Did I receive orders from the orderly Man or did I give him any orders?

ANSWER BY O'HARA:

The orderly man desired you to go on to Temple Patrick or they would not be able to get to Antrim by two o'clock as they were there waiting for him.

EVIDENCE:

Henry Anderson being duly sworn says that he knows the Prisoner, that he the witness was working in his Potatoe field on the morning of the 7th June last and that the Prisoner went up to the house where the witness lived, that he had a Gun on his Shoulder with which he made signs for Witness to come to him, but on his not doing so the Prisoner called to him and on Witness coming to him the Prisoner told him that the Country was up and asked the reason why He the Witness had not joined them. Which the Witness refusing to do, the Prisoner said if he did not his House would be destroyed or words to that effect. Further says that on the same day he saw the Prisoner along with a number of Armed Men on the road leading to Antrim, does not know if whether he had he had any Command of the Party.

QUESTION BY PRISONER:

Do you know if I had any command or whether I was in the Ranks?

ANSWER:

Does not know that the Prisoner had any Command.

QUESTION:

Did you see the Orderly Man coming from Temple Patrick – had he a pike in his hand?

ANSWER:

Does not know what he had in his hand.

EVIDENCE:

Mary Hunter being duly sworn says that on the 7th of June last a number of Persons came to her House in Domrygall and one of them who she was informed his name was John Orr of the Folly, said to her that if she did not turn out her sons her House should be set in a blaze on his coming back. Says said John Orr was armed with a gun and that her Sons did not go with him. Cannot take it upon herself to swear that the Prisoner was the Person that spoke to her.

EVIDENCE:

John English being duly Sworn says he knows the Prisoner, that on the morning of the 7th of June last as he the Witness was passing the Avenue leading down to the Prisoner's House with his Horse and Car, the Prisoner seized his Horse by the head and desired him, the Witness to stop and asked him if he was going to Antrim? On being informed he was, Prisoner replied it would be impossible for him to get there as the Hedges and Ditches were lined with armed Men who would put him to Death. Witness replied if he must be killed it should be near home for he was determined to go to Antrim. Prisoner then declared if he attempted to go he would shoot him himself. Prisoner then left him & witness proceeded to Antrim.

QUESTION:

Had the Prisoner any arms in his hands?

ANSWER:

I saw none with him.

EVIDENCE:

James Kirk being duly sworn, Says he knows the Prisoner, that on the morning of the 7th June last he saw him as he was going into the Town of Antrim and saw him stop the horse and car of John English and desired him, said English, to turn back for that if he proceeded to Antrim he would be shot as the hedges and ditches were lined with armed men. English replied that he would go forward to Antrim, the Prisoner then went down his own avenue and said he would fetch his own gun and shoot him.

QUESTION:

Had the prisoner any arms?

ANSWER:

No he had not.

EVIDENCE:

Question to **Henry O'Hara** the first Witness. Were you at the House of Mary Hunter on the 7th June last?

ANSWER:

I was.

QUESTION:

Did you see the Prisoner there and what conversation passed in your hearing between the Prisoner & Mary Hunter?

ANSWER:

I did, and the Prisoner desired her to turn out her sons or he would set her house in a blaze, On his Oath declares that that the Prisoner was the Man that spoke to Mary Hunter.

The Court having closed the Evidence against the Prisoner adjourned to eleven o'clock the 16th Inst.
16th November: the court met pursuant to Adjournment and proceeded in the Prisoner's Defence.

EVIDENCE:

Henry Anderson examined on the part of the Prisoner, Says he saw the prisoner on the 7th of June last. Did not see him act as an Officer on that day. Saw Henry O'Hara on the 7th June had a conversation with him who were to be Officers on that day and O'Hara made answer that he could not tell until they came to Temple Patrick, Prisoner did not act as on Officer before they came to Temple Patrick as Witness believes, says a person came to the Prisoner while on the road to Temple Patrick and asked him if he was an Officer that day, Prisoner relied that he was not.

QUESTION BY THE COURT:

Did the Prisoner ask you to take a gun or any other arms on the 7th of June?

ANSWER:

Yes the prisoner said he, the Witness should be under Arms on that day.

QUESTION:

> Did you in consequence of what the prisoner said to you take up Arms that day?

ANSWER:

> Yes I did, but I should not have done so had not another party come and said they would take all Men along with them.

EVIDENCE:

> **James Finlay** being duly sworn says he knows the Prisoner. That on the 7th day of June last he saw him near Antrim among a number of armed men, the Prisoner was also armed and were going to Temple Patrick. Says, the Prisoner was applied to take the command but refused to do so. Says the party proceeded to Temple Patrick, and drew up there, and that then the Prisoner fell in on Witnesses right hand and the whole party marched into Antrim, the Prisoner walked in the ranks as a private during the whole time that the Witness was with him. Witness on hearing the report of a Canon made off and went down the Entry and went home to his own house. Witness did not see the Prisoner force any person to join him.

CROSS EXAMINED:

> Will not take upon himself to swear that the prisoner had not the command after he left him. Prisoner did not make Witness a United Irishman, Witness did not see the prisoner for 6 or 8 weeks after the battle of Antrim, On his Oath he says his Master the Prisoner kept out of the way for fear of being taken up, and heard it reported and believed it himself that the Prisoner was Dead. Witness was a United Irishman and took the Oath of Allegiance before the 7th June but has not taken it since.

EVIDENCE:

> **James Johnston** being duly sworn says he knows the Prisoner, Says he saw him on the 7th June last along with a party of men armed with Pikes, Pitchforks & the prisoner was armed with a Gun, the party proceeded to Temple Patrick where they met another Party armed with Muskets who took the Prisoner along with them and witness did not see him afterwards. Witness did not see the Prisoner force any person to join the Party.

CROSS EXAMINED:

> Witness was ordered out by one James Burnet and was given a pitchfork by him, says that the prisoner joined the party with muskets without being forced, Witness did not see the Prisoner from the 7th June until the day he was taken up and believes the prisoner kept out of the way for fear of being taken, has heard it reported that the prisoner was dead but could not form a belief whether he was or not. On his oath it was not the Prisoner that made

him a United Irishman. Witness did not take the benefit of Proclamation that was issued after the Battle of Antrim nor did he take the Oath of Allegiance since.

EVIDENCE:

Colonel Sinclare of the 22nd Regiment of Light Dragoon being duel sworn, says he does not know the Prisoner, has seen Henry O'Hara once or twice from what he knows of him he thinks him a Man to be believed on his Oath in an Court of Justice.

QUESTION:

Did Henry O'Hara confess before you to have received a sum of money for a false prosecution?

ANSWER:

He never did.

QUESTION:

Did not O'Hara ever confess to you his having received any money for a false Prosecution?

ANSWER:

He never did.

EVIDENCE:

Robert Kirk being duly sworn says he knows the Prisoner and saw him on the 7th day of June last, was along with the Prisoner and his party on that day heard the Prisoner refuse to head the Party. Further says that he was at the house of a woman whose name he does not know but who lives at Loughermore and that part called to her to turn out the men of her house, on which she made the answer that they were gone before.

EVIDENCE:

Jane Lees being duly sworn, Says she knows the prisoner and that she saw him in Antrim on the 7th of June armed with a gun, there was a large party of men along with him who were armed with pikes, guns & pitchforks, the Prisoner did not appear to witness to be a leader or officer as he walked among the common men, Says she saw the prisoner for about 15 minutes, it was near the Meeting House.

CROSS EXAMINED:

Cannot take upon herself to swear that the Prisoner was not a leader or Officer in the Town of Antrim after the Battle begun.

The Prisoner having produced an Affidavit stating the absence of a material witness, the Court having taken the same into its consideration indulged the prisoner with time to produce his witness until eleven o'clock the 17th Inst. adjourned.

17th November The Court met pursuant to Adjournment.

EVIDENCE:

The **Rev. George McCartney** being duly sworn, Says he knows Henry O'Hara, never found any inconsistency in his conversation in giving evidence against many persons who were concerned in the Rebellion, believes O'Hara ought to be believed on his Oath in a Court of Justice. Does not know of his own knowledge that the prisoner was a leader in the Rebellion, nor does not know that he was in Antrim on 7th of June last. Further says that the Prisoner sent his sons to him, this Witness, to surrender himself up which Witness refused and sent word by the Prisoner's sons for the Prisoner to surrendered himself to General Goldie.

The Court having heard the Evidence against the Prisoner as also his Defence are of opinion that he is Guilty of the Crimes laid to his Charge and do therefore adjudge him to be hanged by the neck until he is dead at such time and place as Major General Goldie shall be pleased to appoint.

Signed
WILLIAM ANDERTON MAJOR & PRESIDENT
FFOLLIOT WHITEWAY
Deputy Judge Advocate

Appendix IV
The Will of William Orr
of Farranshane

This transcript of William Orr's will is taken from a copy which was in the possession of Nelson Montgomery of Islandreagh. Marked on front is 'copy: Date of issue 12 November 1872.'

THE LAST WILL AND TESTAMENT OF WILLIAM ORR.

I William Orr of Farinshane in the Parish & County of Antrim do make this my last will and testament in manner following viz.

1st I bequeath to my two sons Samuel & John all my landed property in Farinshane which was willed to me by my father to be divided equally & share & share alike by my executors between them as they come of age. And in case of my said two sons shall die before he comes of age, his share shall devolve to the other.

2nd I leave to my three daughters Jane, Alice & Isabella fifty pounds each to be paid to them as they come to twenty one years of age respectively.

3rd As my dear wife is now pregnant - in case she shall have a son & said son live untill he arrive to twenty one years, I leave to him one third part of my lands in Farinshane aforesaid to be then given to him by my executors & taken from the shares of my two sons Samuel & John an equal portion from each's; And if my wife has a daughter, said daughter is at twenty one years to get fifty pound. I appoint that the above sums to my daughters shall be paid out of my landed property by my sons share and share alike.

4th I appoint that my wife untill the time of executing the above bequests arives shall live in & have the benefits of the aforesaid lands in Farinshane and also the property left to me by my father at Toome to be used for her own & my childrens support & maintenance & in case my wife does not choose to live in Farinshane, I allow said place to be left by my executors and the profits arising therefrom to go to my wife & children as aforesaid. But if my wife shall marry during the time above alluded to then & in that case she shall loose all benifits arising from this my last will & my children be taken into the care & management of my Executors. If my wife remain unmarried after the above bequests are paid off, she is to have yearly from her sons then living or holding the land of Farinshane eight pounds to be paid during her widow-hood.

Lastly I allow all my personal property to be divided between my wife & children in equal shares. I appoint Messrs John Greer of Duneane & James Orr of Randalstown & the Revd Alexander Montgomery of Antrim Executors of this my last will.

Signed sealed and published as my will this 4th day of Oct. 1797.
     WM ORR (Seal)

In presence of Alexr Montgomery, James Orr, Josias Wilson.

Administration of the goods and so forth (with the last will and testament) of William Orr late of Farinshane in the County of Antrim deceased were granted by the Consistorial Court of Down and Connor on the 28th day of February 1815 to Isabella Orr the lawful widow and relict of said deceased, The Revd Alexander Montgomery the surviving Executor having duly renounced.

Effects sworn to £135 - 14 -6.

Appendix V
Orr Family Trees

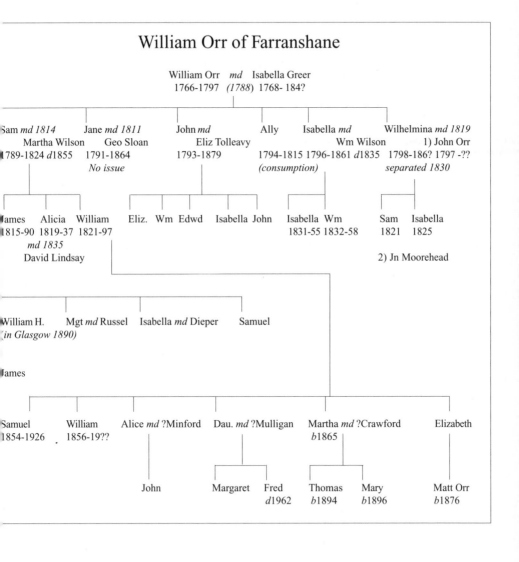

William Orr of Farranshane

William Orr   *md*   Isabella Greer
1766-1797 *(1788)* 1768- 184?

Sam *md 1814*   Jane *md 1811*   John *md*   Ally   Isabella *md*   Wilhelmina *md 1819*
Martha Wilson   Geo Sloan   Eliz Tolleavy   Wm Wilson   1) John Orr
789-1824 *d*1855   1791-1864   1793-1879   1794-1815 1796-1861 *d*1835   1798-186? 1797 -??
                    No issue   *(consumption)*   *separated 1830*

James   Alicia   William   Eliz. Wm Edwd Isabella John   Isabella Wm   Sam   Isabella
1815-90 1819-37 1821-97   1831-55 1832-58   1821   1825
md 1835
David Lindsay   2) Jn Moorehead

William H.   Mgt *md* Russel   Isabella *md* Dieper   Samuel
(in Glasgow 1890)

James

Samuel   William   Alice *md* ?Minford   Dau. *md* ?Mulligan   Martha *md* ?Crawford   Elizabeth
1854-1926   1856-19??   *b*1865

              John   Margaret   Fred   Thomas   Mary   Matt Orr
                                         *d*1962   *b*1894   *b*1896   *b*1876
                              *b*1894 *b*1896

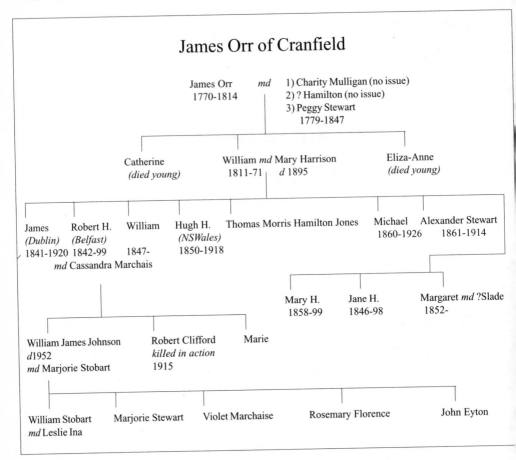

James Orr of Cranfield

James Orr
1770-1814
md
1) Charity Mulligan (no issue)
2) ? Hamilton (no issue)
3) Peggy Stewart
1779-1847

Catherine
(died young)

William *md* Mary Harrison
1811-71 | d 1895

Eliza-Anne
(died young)

James
(Dublin)
1841-1920

Robert H.
(Belfast)
1842-99

William
1847-
md Cassandra Marchais

Hugh H.
(NSWales)
1850-1918

Thomas Morris Hamilton Jones

Michael
1860-1926

Alexander Stewart
1861-1914

Mary H.
1858-99

Jane H.
1846-98

Margaret *md* ?Slade
1852-

William James Johnson
*d*1952
md Marjorie Stobart

Robert Clifford
killed in action
1915

Marie

William Stobart
md Leslie Ina

Marjorie Stewart

Violet Marchaise

Rosemary Florence

John Eyton

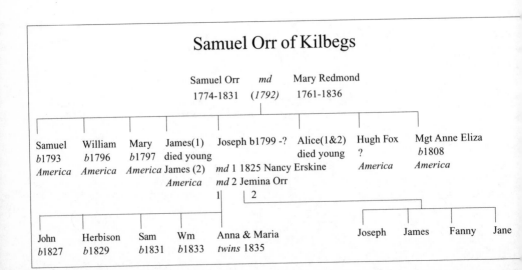

Samuel Orr of Kilbegs

Samuel Orr
1774-1831
md
(1792)
Mary Redmond
1761-1836

Samuel
*b*1793
America

William
*b*1796
America

Mary
*b*1797
America

James(1)
died young
James (2)
America

Joseph b1799 -?

md 1 1825 Nancy Erskine
md 2 Jemina Orr
1| |2

Alice(1&2)
died young

Hugh Fox
?
America

Mgt Anne Eliza
*b*1808
America

John
*b*1827

Herbison
*b*1829

Sam
*b*1831

Wm
*b*1833

Anna & Maria
twins 1835

Joseph

James

Fanny

Jane

John Orr of The Folly

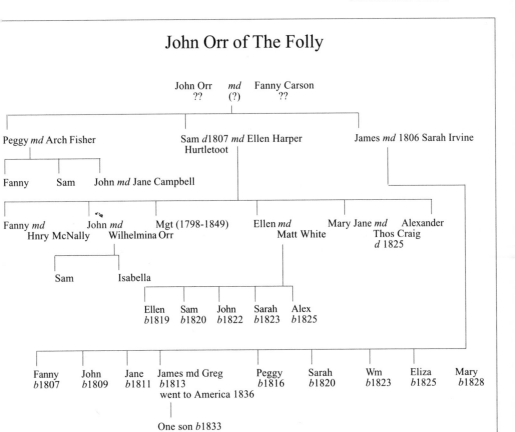

John Orr   *md*   Fanny Carson
??   (?)   ??

Peggy *md* Arch Fisher   Sam *d*1807 *md* Ellen Harper   James *md* 1806 Sarah Irvine
Hurtletoot

Fanny   Sam   John *md* Jane Campbell

Fanny *md*   John *md*   Mgt (1798-1849)   Ellen *md*   Mary Jane *md*   Alexander
Hnry McNally   Wilhelmina Orr   Matt White   Thos Craig
                                                               d 1825

Sam   Isabella

Ellen   Sam   John   Sarah   Alex
*b*1819   *b*1820   *b*1822   *b*1823   *b*1825

Fanny   John   Jane   James md Greg   Peggy   Sarah   Wm   Eliza   Mary
*b*1807   *b*1809   *b*1811   *b*1813   *b*1816   *b*1820   *b*1823   *b*1825   *b*1828
                                went to America 1836

One son *b*1833

James Orr of Creavery

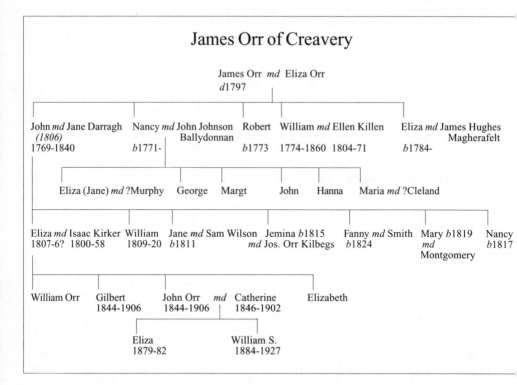

James Orr *md* Eliza Orr
*d*1797

John *md* Jane Darragh   Nancy *md* John Johnson   Robert   William *md* Ellen Killen   Eliza *md* James Hughes
(1806)   Ballydonnan   Magherafelt
1769-1840   *b*1771-   *b*1773   1774-1860 1804-71   *b*1784-

Eliza (Jane) *md* ?Murphy   George   Margt   John   Hanna   Maria *md* ?Cleland

Eliza *md* Isaac Kirker William   Jane *md* Sam Wilson Jemina *b*1815   Fanny *md* Smith Mary *b*1819   Nancy
1807-6? 1800-58   1809-20 *b*1811   *md* Jos. Orr Kilbegs *b*1824   *md*   *b*1817
                                                                                                          Montgomery

William Orr   Gilbert   John Orr   *md*   Catherine   Elizabeth
              1844-1906   1844-1906 | 1846-1902

                    Eliza   William S.
                    1879-82   1884-1927

Bibliography

Allen, A.W. & Gaston, R. (1995) *Inscriptions at St Saviour's Parish Church, Connor. Ballymena Borough Gravestone Series: 4.* Ballymena Borough Council, Ballymena.

Anon (1819 & 1820). Cursory remarks on board the Friendship. *The Asiatic Journal* Vol. VIII pages 237-9, 344-7, 452-6 & 555-8 & Vol. IX pages 37-40, 130-4, 255-8, 451-6 & 564-9.

Anon (1993) *Carmavy Graveyard 1993* ACER, Belfast BT9 6JH.

Anon (1998). *The 1798 rebellion as recorded in the diaries of Gracehill Moravian Church.* Moravian History Magazine, Newtownabbey BT36 7TU.

Bateson, C. *Australian shipwrecks (Vol. one 1622-1850).* A.H & A.W. Reed, Sydney.

Bigger F.J. (1906) *Remember Orr.* Maunsel, Dublin. (Also facsimile reprint (1998) published by United Irishmen Commemoration Committee. ISBN 1 870157 31 1.)

Bush, R. & Rohatgi, P. (1979) *Prints of South-East Asia in the India Office Library.* HMSO, London

Clifford, B. (1992). *Prison adverts and potatoe diggings.* Athol Books, Belfast.

Clutton, C., Baillie, G.H. & Ilbert, C.A.(1973) *Brittens old clocks and watches and their makers.* Eyre Methuen, London.

Curtin, N. (1994) *The United Irishmen. Popular politics in Ulster and Dublin 1791-1798.* Oxford University Press, Oxford.

Day, A. & McWilliams, P. (1995) *Ordnance Survey of Ireland. Parishes of Co. Antrim XI. 1832-2, 1835-9, Antrim Town and Ballyclare.* Institute of Irish Studies, Belfast.

Dickson, C. (1960) *Revolt in the North. Antrim and Down in 1798.* Clonmer & Reynolds, Dublin

Dunlop, E. (compiler) (1993) *William Stavely.* Mid-Antrim Historical Group, Ballymena.

Elliot, M. (1982) *Partners in revolution: The United Irishmen and France.* Yale, New Haven & London.

Foy, R.H. (1989) *Dear uncle. Immigrant letters to Antrim from the USA 1843-1852.* Antrim & District Historical Society, Antrim.

Glendinning, R. (editor) (1996) *Celebrating 400 years 1596-1996 All Saints Parish Church, Antrim.* All Saints Church of Ireland, Antrim.

Hall, D. (1998) *A battle lost and won.* The author, Antrim. ISBN 0 9532967 0 9.

Hughes, G. (1996) *Hewn from the rock. The story of First Antrim Presbyterian Church.* The session and committee of First Antrim Presbyterian Church, Antrim.

Kavanagh, A. (1998) *The aftermath of the rebellion.* In Forde, W. (ed.) *Shemalier '98 A history of Castlebridge, Screen and Curracloe in 1798.* pp 49-53.

Kenny, J.G. (1988) *As the crow flies over rough terrain.* Published by the author, 'The Cottage' 61 Parade Road, Ballygarvey, Ballymena BT43 7JZ..

Killen, J. (1997) *The decade of the United Irishmen. Contemporary accounts 1791-1801.* The Blackstaff Press, Belfast.

Killen, W.D. (1901) *Reminiscences of a long life.* Hodder & Stoughton, London. Also facsimile reprint (1995) published by the Braid Books and Moyola Books (ISBN 1 873401 13 2).

Lecky, W.E.H. (1892) *A history of Ireland in the eighteenth century* Longmans, London.

Leslie, J.B (1993) *Clergy of Connor since Patrician times.* Ulster Historical Foundation, Belfast.

McCollum, R. (1994) *The life of John Paul.* In: Stewart, I. (compiler) *Loughmorne Presbyterian Church, graveyard and surrounding district.* pp 3-9.

McNeill, M. (1988) *The life and times of Mary Ann McCracken 1760-1866.* The Blackstaff Press, Belfast.

Mac Suibhne, B. (1998) Up but not out: Why did north-west Ulster not rise in 1798. In Póirtéir, C (ed.) *The great Irish rebellion of 1798.* Mercier, Dublin, pp 83-100

Madden, R.R. (undated) *Antrim and Down in '98. The lives of Henry Joy McCracken, Henry Munro, James Hope, William Putnam McCabe and Rev. James Porter.* Cameron & Ferguson Edition.

Madden, R.R. (1858) *The United Irishmen - Their lives and times.* Fourth series, second edition. James Duffy, Dublin.

Majury, M. (1936) *The First Antrim Presbyterian Church 'Something attempted, something done': Gleanings from over 300 years of Presbyterianism in Antrim.* 28 pp.

Malcomson, A.P.W. (1972) *The extraordinary career of the 2nd Earl of Massereene, 1743-1805.* Her Majesty's Stationery Office, Belfast.

Mills L.A. (1960) Penang 1786-1830. *Journal of the Malaysian Branch of the Royal Asiatic Society* Vol. 33 part 3.

M'Skimmon, S. (1853) *History of the Irish rebellion in the year 1798 particularly in Antrim, Down and Derry.* John Mullan, Belfast

Musgrave R. (1802) *Memoirs of different rebellions in Ireland* Third edition Dublin.

Nicholson, I.H. *Gazetteer of Sydney Shipping 1788-1840.* A Roebuck Book, Canberra ISBN 0 909434 18 2.

Pakenham, T. (1969) *The year of liberty.* Hodder & Stoughton, London.

Power, P.C. (1997?) *The courts martials of 1798-99.* Irish Historical Press, Ireland.

Robinson, K. (1998) *North Down and Ards in 1798.* North Down Heritage Centre, Bangor.

Roebuck P. (editor) (1983) *Macartney of Lisanoure 1737-1806 Essays in biography.*

Smith, W.S. (1888) *Historical gleanings in Antrim and neighbourhood.* Mayne & Boyd, Belfast. (Facsimile reproduction 1983, Area Resource Centre, Antrim)

Smith, W.S. (1996) *Memories of '98.* Mid-Antrim Historical Group, Ballymena.

Smyth, A. (1984) *The story of Antrim.* Antrim Borough Council, Antrim.

Stewart, A.T.Q. (1995) *The summer soldiers, The 1798 rebellion in Antrim and Down.* The Blackstaff Press, Belfast.

Walthen, J. (1814) *Journey of a voyage in 1811 and 1812 to Madras and China.* Bently, London.

Weber, P. (1997) *On the road to rebellion, The United Irishmen and Hamburg 1796-1803.* Four Courts Press, Dublin.

West, T. (1902) *Historical sketch of First Antrim Presbyterian Church prepared for the Coronation Bazaar June 26, 27 and 28, 1902.*

Whitaker, A-M. (1994) *Unfinished revolution.* Crossing Press, Sydney.

Williams, T. (1998) *Two local families intertwined in 1798.* In Forde, W. (ed.) *Shemalier '98 A history of Castlebridge, Screen and Curracloe in 1798.* pp 29-37.

Young, R.M. (1893). *Ulster in '98. Episodes and anecdotes.* Marcus Ward, Belfast.

Index